Cuyahoga Falls

Then & Now

Carolyn Vogenitz

Cuyahoga Falls
Then & Now

Vogenitz, Carolyn, 1937-
Cuyahoga Falls Then & Now

Cuyahoga Falls Then & Now is about Cuyahoga Falls, Ohio, from the time when the Indians inhabited the land to the year 2002. The book includes historical and current information, pictures, and interviews with long-time residents.

Bibliography
Includes Index

1. History. 2. Region. 3. Biography.

Cover Design by Todd Hone
Printed by Towpath Printing Company, Akron, Ohio

Waterside Publishing
3326 Waterside Drive
Akron, OH 44319

Wtsdpub@aol.com

ISBN 0-9670779-1-5

In Appreciation

Special thanks to those who willingly helped with this project. To Liz Cross, Cuyahoga Falls Historical Society Museum Curator, and her devoted staff members, Babette Robinson and Mary Lou Atleson, who were at the museum each time I visited. To Pete Mellinger, who offered boxes of Cuyahoga Falls memorabilia for me to peruse and borrow.

To Georgiana Colvin, who proofread Portage Lakes Then & Now, *and who graciously offered to proofread this book. To Nancy Milford at Taylor Memorial Public Library, to the staff at the Akron-Summit County Public Library for assisting in a variety of ways. And to my husband, Glen, who took dozens of pictures of Cuyahoga Falls as it is today.*

Always when there are many individuals to thank, someone's name is unfortunately omitted. I apologize in advance if I have overlooked anyone. With that said, I am very grateful to the following individuals for sharing information, pictures and interviews.

Thanks to Tim Thomas, John Lambert, Dale Haggarty, Bob Heath, Harry Heath, Keith Haag, Marj Schlaeppi, John Phillips, John Wunderle, Joseph Jesensky, Virginia Bloetcher, Cheryl McFadden, James Stahl, Lucy Bibbee, Donna Daulton, Linda Nye, Lila VanSwerigen, John Seiberling, Bill Clifford, Harding Wichert, Marc Moon, Gene Fordham, Marion Pearce, Bill Parthe, Floriana Hall, Sue Truby, Dick Pierson, Mayor Don Robart, Elizabeth and Dick Hurley, Patricia Gritton, Dorothy Wright, Bee and Walt McLean, Don Miller, Dr. William B. Rogers, Dick Stodghill, Joe Maite, Jeff Iula, Tom Dillon, Jim Ervin, Alma Canfield, Phil Keren, Don Dieterich, Jean and Mike Krieger, Jack Richard, Charles Pilliod Jr., Judge Lynn Slaby, Robert Gallagher, Marlene Shoemaker, Carol Pocock, Elizabeth Cailor, Harold McCready, Lt. Jack Davis, Laura Petrella, Abe J. Moses, Mike Knapp, Bob LeFever, Roger Taylor, Jill Gifford, and Bill Katzenmeyer.

Thanks!

We have read volumes of material published about the Cuyahoga Falls area. We have spent hours at the local libraries and the Cuyahoga Falls Historical Society. We have talked to dozens of community residents and interviewed many long-time residents.

We have discovered there is often more than one version of an event or description of a place. Over the years stories change and even published information does not always agree. Our goal was to be as accurate as possible in recording the information gathered for the book. We have attempted to include what is considered the best-educated version. We have enjoyed the effort. We hope you enjoy the book!

Carolyn

Table of Contents

I

Cuyahoga Falls Profile

2002

*Overview of Cuyahoga Falls
at the Beginning of the Twenty-first Century*

Cuyahoga Falls has the enchantment of a small community, the advantages of city status, and the position of being on the leading edge of middle class expectations. Its growth and development can be traced to industrious visionaries who provided strong leadership. Its citizens are hard working individuals with realistic goals.

The community was founded in 1812 and officially incorporated in 1836. By 1868 the bustling commonwealth was large enough to be considered a village. Ohio state law determines that a population of at least 5,000 constitutes city status, and therefore, by 1920 Cuyahoga Falls was automatically considered a city.

The annexation of Northampton Township, 18 square miles, by merger in 1986, tripled the geographical size of Cuyahoga Falls. Today, 27.8 square miles lie within city limits. Located one-mile northeast of Akron, Ohio, and 20 miles south of Cleveland, the city of Cuyahoga Falls is a prime locale for residential and economic growth.

Cuyahoga Falls is the second largest city in Summit County. The population of the city as recorded by the Census Bureau in the year 2000 was 49,374. There are more females than males that call the Falls home. Census figures indicate that there are 25,946 females and 23,428 males living here.

The median age of residents living in Cuyahoga Falls is 37.2. There are 7,963 individuals that are 65 years of age or older, and 817 that are 85 years of age or older.

Figures on housing units indicate that 68% are single family, 9% are two family, and 23% are multi-family units. How often do folks move? In Cuyahoga Falls, 57.2% have lived in the same house since 1995. The median home value is $106,100, up 35% since 1990.

The median household income for 1999 was $42,263, up 5.4% from 1989 figures. Census numbers indicate that only 6.1% are considered in poverty, down from the 6.6% recorded for 1989. Of the individuals 25 years of age and older, 25.6% have at least a Bachelor's Degree.

Municipally owned and operated electric, water and sanitation utilities provide consumer rates that are lower than those of surrounding communities. Citywide recycling, efficient snow removal and the City Ecology Center serve the residents.

A Charter form of government was instituted in 1960, with a Mayor and an eleven-member City Council elected by the voters. The Cuyahoga Falls Municipal Court serves sixteen communities and handles traffic, criminal and civil cases.

Local police and fire departments oversee community safety. Cuyahoga Falls General Hospital is located within city limits. Numerous clubs and organizations provide ample opportunity for citizens to pursue special interests. Public and private schools are available.

Recreational facilities within Cuyahoga Falls are outstanding for a city of approximately 50,000 residents. The Parks and Recreation Department oversees Water Works Family Aquatic Center, the Natatorium, Brookledge Golf Club, Downview Sports Center, the Golf Academy, Quirk Cultural Center, Falls River Tours, several indoor rental facilities, and 24 community/school parks.

Brief histories and information about Northampton Township and Silver Lake are included in *Cuyahoga Falls Then & Now.* Since Northampton is now Ward 8 of the city, and Silver Lake abuts Cuyahoga Falls on its eastern border, it is difficult to separate events and happenings based upon political boundaries.

Blossom Music Center, the Porthouse Theatre, and 6,000 acres of the Cuyahoga Valley National Recreation Area lie within the borders of the city. Those seeking entertainment, cultural events, or the opportunity to enjoy nature, surely can satisfy their desires without traveling far from home.

A city that is nearly 200 years old obviously has a fascinating and varied history. Many of the stories have been told over and over again. This book, *Cuyahoga Falls Then & Now*, recalls some of the most important people, places and events; however, it also informs the reader of recent history and current situations.

Historically, the use of the land identified as Cuyahoga Falls can be divided into five eras. Beginning with the *Indian Era*, the land was used primarily for hunting, fishing and transportation via the Cuyahoga River and well known paths. Next came the arrival of the white man, or the *Early Settlers Era*, when land was made available through land grants and investment entrepreneurs.

Because of its location on a river with ample power to drive mills, Cuyahoga Falls entered the *Milling & Manufacturing Era*. In the early to mid 1900s, location near the rapidly growing industrial belt pressed the community into what is identified as the *Bedroom Community Era*. Today, Cuyahoga Falls is in the *Expansion Era*, with rapid business and residential growth due to the merger of Northampton Township.

II

Awakening of the Land
Glaciers, Indians,
Trails, Mary Campbell's Cave,
Signal Tree

Before the White Man

Long before the well-recognized Nations of Native American Indians occupied the Western Hemisphere, small bands of prehistoric Indians roamed the land. The nomadic groups were scavengers who moved from place to place hunting and gathering food for survival.

During the Pleistocene Period several glaciers left the Great Lakes region with steep hills and ravines. The five Great Lakes were carved out during the surge and recession of the slow moving ice. As the ice sheets retreated, the deep voids were filled with meltwater. The geological turmoil left this part of the country with heaps of clay, sand, gravel, and huge outcroppings of rock. Virginia Kendall Park, the Gorge and the summit (or watershed divide) are examples of the devastation left behind.

Approximately forty miles south of Lake Erie, running at an east-west angle through the state, is a ridge of rock that dictates direction for the rivers and streams in the area. Geologists prefer to call it a watershed divide, but often it is referred to as a continental divide or the Ohio Divide. This rocky ridge runs through Akron in the general vicinity of Summit Lake. To give you an idea of the height of this divide, James Geddes, the engineer employed to plan the building of the Ohio Erie Canal in the 1820s, reported that Summit Lake in Akron was 404 feet above Lake Erie.

All rivers and tributaries north of the divide flow into the Great Lakes-Saint Lawrence Watershed by way of Lake Erie. The water continues through the St. Lawrence Seaway, and finally empties into the Atlantic Ocean. Rivers and tributaries on the other side of the divide flow south toward the Ohio River. Water that has traveled hundreds of miles pours into the mighty Mississippi River and eventually dumps into the Gulf of Mexico.

Prehistoric Indians known as the Paleos, Archaic, Adenas, and Hopewells left traces of habitation dating back to 7,000 B.C. The Paleos and Archaid groups were strictly nomadic and moved often. It is believed, however, that the Adena and Hopewell Indians moved less frequently and actually grew crops in fertile valleys and along riverbanks.

The Adena and Hopewell Indians also practiced the custom of building earthen mounds and are referred to as the Mound Builders. Archeologists have determined that the mounds had a variety of purposes. Some were used as burial grounds, while others may have played a part in religious or spiritual ceremonies.

It is believed that some of the dirt and rock compositions, regardless of how impressive looking, may simply have served as strongholds or lookout points for the tribe.

Glacial turmoil left this part of the state with clay, sand, gravel, and huge outcroppings of beautiful rock.
Photo Courtesy of Taylor Memorial Library

Ohio has been referred to as the *Mound Builder State* because of the estimated 10,000 ancient mounds located throughout the state. Most traces of large mounds are found in central and southern Ohio. The Serpent Mound of Chillicothe, Ohio, and Alligator Mound in Newark, Ohio, are effigy mounds.

However, archeologists have found remnants of somewhat smaller mounds in the Cuyahoga River Valley, with more than thirty mounds in Summit County alone. Valley View Golf Club on Cuyahoga Street boasts one of the largest mounds in the area. Chances are that most golfers do not recognize the forty-foot high hill covered with oak trees as an ancient Indian mound.

According to what is presently known, the Mound Builders were gone when the Native American Indians began arriving in the Cuyahoga Valley. A variety of opinions concerning their exodus continue to be debated within the archeological community nationwide.

Unfortunately, numerous mound sites have been destroyed and lost forever with the building of highways, shopping malls and housing developments. Ongoing research by historians and archeologists becomes more difficult as time passes.

* * *

Native American Indians

Dropping elm bark canoes and dugouts into the meandering crooked river, the Indians paddled as far as possible toward preconceived destinations. When the water would no longer transport them, they carried their vessels and other belongings over the well-traveled portage to the next body of flowing water.

The river we call the Cuyahoga was an important landmark for it provided a means of travel and allowed the Indians to move from one place to another with relative ease. Approximately 100 miles in length, this famous waterway flows both north and south. Its headwater is located in Hambden Township in Geauga County. It runs south and then makes a "U" turn near what is now Merriman Road and Portage Path, and it finally empties into Lake Erie in Cleveland.

Historians agree that the Indians called it the *crooked river*. Writers tell us that the Mohawks called the river *Cayagaga;* the Senecas referred to it as the *Cayohaga;* and the Delaware Indians called it the *Diohaga* or *Kayhoga*. As Indian pronunciations were translated into the English language, the spelling of Cuyahoga had nearly as many variations as the river had waterfalls.

The Iroquois Indians formed a confederation of Five Nations in around 1570. By right of conquest, they claimed a large parcel of land that was equal to about six or seven states.

The English referred to the eastern section of the parcel of land as the Black Forest. It ran from what is now Pittsburgh, Pennsylvania, to the western border of Indiana. It is believed that the forest was very dense and probably few Late Woodland Indians actually stayed in the Cuyahoga Valley area until after 1700.

One must take into consideration the arrival of the white man in the New World to understand Indian history. The encroachment of the settlers and the aggressive stance taken by the government caused the Indians in the east to move westward.

Groups of displaced Indians came into the Cuyahoga Valley, and small Indian villages began to appear on the banks of the "crooked river". The valley provided fertile soil for planting, and the woods were full of animals for the hunt.

It is believed that the Indians may have lived in one location for seven to ten years and then moved to a new site to improve their living conditions. The new place might have been only a mile from the original village.

There were several reasons to move a camp. Sanitation was sometimes a concern, and when camps were no longer healthy, the Indians would pick up their belongings and relocate. Another issue was the availability of firewood. Downed timber was harvested for the ongoing campfires, and when it became necessary to go long distances to gather wood, consideration was given to moving to another site.

Nations, often referred to as *tribes*, believed to be in what we now call the Cuyahoga Valley, were the Seneca (who were mainly part of the Iroquois Nation), the Delaware, the Mingo, and the Ottawa.

The information concerning groups of Indians that lived in the general area of what is now Cuyahoga Falls, from approximately 1700 to 1800, comes from diaries, ledgers, historical archives, recorded narratives, archaeologists interested in Indian research, and *a great deal of folklore*.

It would seem that we should have volumes of information about the people who lived on the land within the last few centuries. We do have stories, speculation and constantly changing opinions about the previous inhabitants. However, the Native American Indians did not have a written language or alphabet. Tribes had *storytellers* who were responsible for history, legends and tales. Common practice was for information to be passed on by word of mouth.

In addition, two or three centuries ago, the ability to read and write among the white population was limited to a select group of people. There were, of course, schools in the larger towns for children of the wealthy class. However, often individuals were home schooled or received only a few years of formal education, especially in the untamed new west.

Unfortunately, today we know that many old maps and diaries thought to be precious documents have been found to contain conflicting information. With that in mind we share with the reader the following *facts and folklore* about the Indians in Cuyahoga Falls, Silver Lake and the Cuyahoga Valley.

* * *

Chiefs and Their Indian Villages

Chief Pontiac – Ottawa Village – The "Tiger of the Northwest" spent time in a village on the west side of the Cuyahoga River near what is now Boston Heights.

Lack of recorded information makes it hard to identify the exact location, and some historians believe it was near the intersection of the present Columbia and Riverview Roads. Geographer and surveyor Lewis Evans' Map of 1755 names the village Tawas, probably an abbreviation of Ottawa. It was later known as Ponty's Camp.

Pontiac was born around 1720, near what is now Detroit, Michigan, to a Chippewa Indian mother and an Ottawa Indian chief. His Indian name was Obwandiyag and pronounced Bwon-dioc in the Ottawa language. He was a respected War Chief and had the power to organize and lead war parties.

Pontiac always favored the French who had been in the territory and were trading with the Indians and supplying them with guns and ammunition. The French and Indian War against the British was a violent struggle. Chief Pontiac was successful in organizing a confederacy of many tribes of Indians who participated in warfare from 1763-65.

It was obvious that the British forces were stronger, and the French were not able to offer the support Pontiac needed. In 1766 Chief Pontiac signed a peace treaty at Oswego, New York. He probably returned to the Cuyahoga Valley occasionally, but he eventually settled near the Maumee River in Ohio.

An Indian from Illinois murdered him in 1769. Some historians believe the Indian was Black Dog who was paid by the British to eliminate Chief Pontiac.

Chief Logan - Mingo Village – A village at the intersection of Yellow Creek and Riverview Roads owed its allegiance to one of the most famous Mingo Indian Chiefs.

He was a remarkable, peace loving man who had been given the name of Logan because of his father's friendship with James Logan of Pennsylvania. Logan's Indian name was Tachnechdorus. He was born in Pennsylvania in about 1725 of Iroquois parents, and when he was approximately 45 years old, he moved his family to Ohio.

Logan remained friendly with the whites until 1774, when a group of settlers murdered his family. He became an angry, bitter individual who often raided white settlements revenging the death of his loved ones. The Mingo Nation eventually scattered throughout Ohio.

Chief Logan was invited to attend a peacekeeping meeting near Chillicothe. He refused the invitation and delivered instead an emotional message concerning the relationship between the Indians and the settlers. The message berated the whites for their mistreatment of the Indians.

Chief Logan was murdered near what is now Detroit in 1780. The Ohio Historical Society maintains Logan's Elm Memorial south of Circleville, Ohio.

Chief Stigwanish - Seneca Village – With his band of people he farmed the river bottoms. Settlers were known to purchase corn grown by the Indians on 30 or 40 acres of property near what is now Brandywine Golf Course.

18

Stigwanish was a friend of David Hudson, who established the first white settlement in what is now Summit County. The Chief's friendly ways caused problems with other Indian groups, and the settlers built a blockhouse for him to use in the case of an emergency.

He was a good-looking, six-foot tall individual who had the reputation of drinking too much alcohol. He gave up the habit after an incident that resulted in shame and sorrow. In a drunken rage, he threw a tomahawk at his wife and killed the young papoose she carried on her back; or so the story goes.

Chief Wabmong – Mingo Village – Two Mingo Villages were located in the Silver Lake area. One was northwest of the lake near what is now Route 59. The other, a much larger encampment, was located near the lake called Wetmore (or Stow Pond) in the early 1800s. Approximately, 500 Mingo Indians lived where the Mahoning Trail separated the village from the lake, under the leadership of Chief Wabmong.

Mingo Indians lived peacefully among the whites for several years. A settler, Mrs. William Wetmore, befriended the Indians and taught some of them how to sew clothing from material traded for skins and furs. The Indians shared nature's remedies for scurvy, malaria, typhus, and typhoid with the appreciative settlers.

The British bribed Mingo warriors and tried to encourage them to murder the whites living in Stow Township. The story is told that Chief Wabmong stopped the massacre and moved his entire village from the region overnight.

Chief Net-a-wat-wees – Delaware Villages - The Delaware Indians were also known as the Leni-Lenape, and they were called the *Grandfather Nation* by other Indians. They belonged to the Algonquin linguistic family, one of the major Indian languages of the time. Within their nation were the Turtle (or Tortoise), Turkey, and Wolf (or Monsey) Clans.

Chief Net-a-wat-wees was chief of the Turtle Clan. He had three villages in the region: One at the mouth of the river near Valley View Golf Course; the second on Smith Road not far from a Mingo Indian Camp; and the third, a temporary location, was the famous Mary Campbell's Cave. The permanent camp was eventually located on the north side of the river close to where the Ohio Edison Dam was later built.

Delaware Indians were generally thought to be peaceful. However, they too became resentful at times and created havoc among the settlers. It was in late 1758 or early 1759 when a raiding party, probably led by Chief Net-a-wat-wees, traveled to the Pennsylvania area and captured a white woman, Mrs. Stuart, and young girl by the name of Mary Campbell.

Chief Net-a-wat-wees adopted Mary and treated her as a member of his family. She remained with the Indians for approximately seven years. She was returned to her family, at Colonel Boquet's camp, when the Indians released 81 men and 125 women and children who had been taken captive during the French and Indian War.

✳ ✳ ✳

Getting to the Valley

Two important trails brought the Indians and eventually the white settlers to the Cuyahoga Valley. The first was the well-worn Mahoning (or Watershed Trail) coming west from Pennsylvania. It ran north of the present day Youngstown, Ohio, and crossed the upper Cuyahoga River near what is now the city of Kent.

When it reached what eventually became Stow Township, it split, and one branch of the trail came into

20

what is now the city of Cuyahoga Falls near what is now Portage Trail.

At that point the Mahoning Trail intersected with another important path. The north-south trail, known for years as Portage Path, led travelers to the important Tuscarawas River. In this part of the rugged terrain, the meandering Cuyahoga River and the Tuscarawas River were only eight miles apart. Travel was difficult, but getting to the available waterway was the accepted plan. It was necessary to portage (or carry) canoes and belongings over the deeply rutted path.

Just north of Long Lake in Coventry Township the Indians could drop their canoes into the water of the Tuscarawas River. The river, a tributary of the Muskingum River, would eventually take them to the mighty Ohio River. From there they could reach the Mississippi River and eventually the Gulf of Mexico.

In the fall of 2001, two bronze statues were erected to mark the beginning and ending points of the portage taken by the Indians. The current route was resurveyed using the original notes as recorded by Moses Warren in 1791.

The bronze eight-foot identical statues are of an American Indian carrying a canoe. American Indian, Peter Jones, of the Beaver Clan of the Onondaga Tribe, was the artist chosen to design and build the sculptures.

One of the statues stands at the northern end of the portage next to the Cuyahoga River at Merriman Road and North Portage Path. The second statue stands at the southern tip of the path near Young's Restaurant on Manchester Road. A series of 31 bronze arrowhead shaped markers designate the trail.

The portage from north to south runs through Sand Run Metropolitan Park, crosses Copley Road, and continues through Perkins Park. It crosses Euclid Avenue heading towards Wooster Avenue and Manchester Road.

The trail then crosses Waterloo Road and terminates near Young's Restaurant on the Tuscarawas River.

William Yeck, a Dayton, Ohio advertising executive and philanthropist, grew up in the Akron area. He initiated the $500,000 project and provided the majority of the necessary funding through the William & Dorothy Yeck Family Foundation.

In 2001, eight-foot tall statues were erected to memorialize the 8.5-mile Portage Path used by the Indians. The 4000-pound bronze statue marking the northern end of the trail is at Merriman Road and North Portage Path. An identical statue stands at the south end of the path on the banks of the Tuscarawas River near Young's Restaurant on Manchester Road.

Mary Campbell Cave

Take a hike down the tree-covered path in Gorge Park, and stop below the massive cliff that was once called Old Maid's Kitchen. It is known that Mrs. Fosdick's Tavern was located on the plateau above the cave during horse and buggy days. The tavern's famous fried chicken dinners and the lovely picnic site nearby made it a favorite spot to visit.

It is believed that a girl by the name of Mary Campbell was kidnapped in Pennsylvania by the Delaware Indians and held temporarily here until the permanent Indian camp was ready.

The overhanging cliff has a history that precedes Mrs. Fosdick's Tavern. The Daughters of the American Revolution changed the name of the cave in memory of the young pioneer girl who had been captured by the

Indians. Mary Campbell Cave is believed to be the site of a temporary camp used by Chief Net-a-wat-wees and the Delaware Indians.

Mary Campbell and a family friend, Mrs. Stuart, were kidnapped from their home in Cumberland County, Pennsylvania, and brought to the Cuyahoga Valley area. Historians disagree on Mary's exact age. Some believe she was seven years old when taken captive; others say she was twelve years old. One thing upon which they all agree, is that the Delaware Indian Chief Net-a-wat-wees favored Mary, and treated her as a daughter.

In 1764, at the end of the French & Indian War, about 60 miles south of Akron, near what is now Coshocton, prisoners were released. Mary was reunited with her family, and returned to Pennsylvania.

* * *

The Signal Tree

The centuries old Bur Oak (*Quercus Macrocarpa*) tree is actually located in the Cascade Valley Metro Park. In addition to its shape, the tree is of importance because it is believed to be near the place where canoes were pulled from the Cuyahoga River to be carried over the eight-mile portage heading south.

It was customary for Indians to bend and shape trees to mark paths that would serve as nature's maps to those traveling in uncharted lands. There is no documentation about the origin of this tree's shape, but it is agreed that nature must have had some assistance from humans.

Referred to as the *Signal Tree* since the early 1800s, the tree is approximately 300 years old and showing significant signs of weakness. Supported by metal guy wires, the fragile old man of the forest sits alone now in an open field.

The massive four-foot trunk supports two arm like branches on either side. Both extend approximately 13 feet horizontally before turning sharply upward. Over 100 feet tall, with an average spread of 75 feet, the majestic old tree still fascinates visitors with its candelabrum-like shape.

A bit of mystique surrounds the observer standing before the lofty giant. Those with imagination have visions of Indians moving about in this same area hundreds of years ago. Some visitors are a bit skeptical because the river is a good distance from the *Signal Tree* and it is hard to understand what help the tree may have been to the traveling Indians. Other visitors truly believe that the tree did indeed serve as a directional for Indians moving through the area.

Standing in a grassy field at Cascade Valley Metro Park, the centuries old Bur Oak "Signal Tree" may have been purposely shaped by Indians to let travelers know that they had reached the northern terminus of the Portage Path and the Cuyahoga River.

Indians of Today

Historical accounts tell us that most Indians left this part of Ohio by 1812. Yet we know there are Native American Indians that reside here in Summit County today. How did that happen?

Sally Thomas, Program Coordinator at the *North American Indian Cultural Center,* on Triplett Boulevard in Akron, Ohio, explained when and how some of the Indians arrived in Ohio.

In the 1950s, a United States government program was initiated that relocated Indians from reservations to urban areas. It was assumed that a better way of life was possible if the Indians were in an area where jobs, housing, and education were available. In the state of Ohio the cities that received "Indian transplants" were Cleveland, Cincinnati, Columbus, Dayton, and Toledo.

The *Cultural Center* tell us that there are 34 Nations (sometimes referred to as tribes) represented in Ohio. There are 450 Nations represented throughout the contiguous United States.

The U. S. 2000 Census figures indicate that 25,000 "card carrying" Native American Indians live in the state of Ohio. There are another 250,000 Ohioans that claim Indian Heritage.

A "card carrying" Indian is a person that has proven through "Blood Quantum" that he or she is an Indian. How is Blood Quantum determined? Each Indian Nation sets guidelines for its own "Blood Quantum". Using these guidelines when a request from an individual is received, the Nation then decides if the person claiming Indian heritage qualifies.

How many Native American Indians reside in Summit County? According to the 2000 Census, there are 1,065. We are assuming that some of them live in Cuyahoga Falls.

26

III

Those With Vision

*Forefathers, Early Business Ventures,
Damming the Crooked River,
Silver Lake, Northampton*

A view from the Portage Trail Bridge over the Cuyahoga River shows numerous businesses located near the dam in 1916.

Photo Courtesy of Cuyahoga Falls Historical Society

Our ancestors saw hope and promise in a land that offered new opportunities for those willing to take the risk. They came with enthusiasm, determination, a pocket full of change, and an overwhelming amount of *guts*.

We give them credit for challenging the unknown and establishing the groundwork that identified the crooked river location as a prospective site for a viable commerce center.

Much can be said for a community with ample waterpower. Throughout civilization mankind has strived to settle in areas where water flows. Even today, manufacturing relies heavily on the availability of water for factory production and transportation. Industrial cities located within the Great Lakes region have been overwhelmingly successful during the last century.

At the end of the Revolutionary War, aggressive negotiations began for the land that would be claimed and eventually settled. Virginia, Connecticut, Pennsylvania, New York, and Massachusetts were quick to use grants and charters dating as far back as 1606, as rights for grabbing huge tracts of land.

Connecticut had been granted land from the English Crown during the seventeenth century, and tried to use that proclamation to claim a strip of land about 60 miles wide north of the 41st parallel spanning the entire continent.

That attempt was not successful. However, Connecticut was granted a parcel of land 120 miles long between the 41st parallel and the shores of Lake Erie. We now call it the Western Reserve, and it includes approximately 3,000,000 acres of land stretching from the Pennsylvania border to Sandusky Bay. Most of Summit County lies within the Western Reserve.

A group of speculators calling themselves the Connecticut Land Company purchased the tract of land for $1,200,000. The Connecticut General Assembly set aside an additional 500,000 acres of land, referred to as the Fire Lands, at the western edge of the Reserve for Connecticut citizens who had lost their homes during the Revolutionary War.

In 1796, an Act of Congress determined that *a state was to be divided into counties, and the counties subdivided into townships.* Surveyors were hired to divide the unexplored wilderness.

Cuyahoga Falls was a booming little manufacturing center with factories taking advantage of the power of the river.
Photo Courtesy of Taylor Memorial Library

Although the terrain was extremely rugged, the rushing water of the Cuyahoga River was seen as an asset by prospective developers. In 1837, Dr. Eliakim Crosby, of Akron, and several investors planned the *Chuckery Race* that would harness the energy of the Cuyahoga River and provide power to manufacturers.

Crosby had orchestrated the successful Cascade Mill Race in Akron, and he believed that water from the Cuyahoga River could be directed by way of a canal that would benefit the region. The plan involved building a 20-foot dam just below Prospect Avenue in Cuyahoga Falls. A four-mile canal would be constructed terminating near what is now Uhler Avenue in North Akron.

After seven years of hard work, and the investment of hundreds of thousands of dollars, the water flowed for only a few hours. Leaks in the canal bed and reluctance on the part of investors to provide additional money ended the grandiose plans for the *Chuckery Race.*

Summit County was created in 1840 by combining 16 townships (10 from Portage County, 2 from Stark County and 4 from Medina County). The population of the newly formed Summit County was 22,560 according to the census that year.

Citizens of Cuyahoga Falls campaigned vigorously to acquire the honor of being selected the County Seat. Fierce competition between what is now Akron and Cuyahoga Falls ensued. Many expected the Cuyahoga River would be the trump card in determining the location of a thriving metropolis and the coveted County Seat.

State officials wavered numerous times in making a decision between Akron, the north hill area called Summit City, and Cuyahoga Falls. The political arena was a virtual battlefield, and speculation concludes that a small fortune was spent in the ongoing struggle.

Henry Newberry, Elisha Noyes Sill, Birdsey Booth, and other Cuyahoga Falls supporters had put up a good fight. However, on April 5, 1842, when constituents cast their ballots for the location of the County Seat, Akron received 2,978 votes, Cuyahoga Falls 1,384 votes and Summit City 101 votes.

Although not selected to be the honored city, Cuyahoga Falls, five miles north of Akron, continued to develop and grow at an incredible speed. Credit must be given to numerous residents responsible for the expansion and progress of the city. From the early 1800s through today, courageous men and women helped to make the city on the crooked river what it is today.

Forefathers

William Wetmore (1771-1827) was born in Middletown, Connecticut, and hired by Joshua Stow as land agent of property in the Western Reserve (purchased from the Connecticut Land Company). Wetmore moved to Ohio in 1804, and he became one of the original proprietors of Cuyahoga Falls.

He built the second house in what became Stow Township. Wetmore was elected Justice of the Peace of Stow, as well as Clerk of the Court of Ravenna, Ohio. During the War of 1812, he operated a commissary for the troops stationed at Old Portage.

Wetmore and Joshua Stow owned 210 acres, the southern border being Portage Trail, and began developing Cuyahoga Falls in 1825. Wetmore's sons, William, Jr. and Henry, supervised 30 men who constructed a dam, gristmill, sawmill, paper and linseed oil mills.

***

Edward Rowland Sill (1841-1887) was born in Windsor, Connecticut, and was orphaned at 12 years of age. He moved to Cuyahoga Falls to live with his uncle, Elisha Noyes Sill, in a mansion known as the Sill House (on Front Street between what is now Broad Boulevard and Portage Trail).

He attended Exeter Academy and graduated from Yale University. He studied law and for a short time was a student at Harvard Divinity School. In a trip to Cuyahoga Falls in 1867, Edwin fell in love with and married his cousin, Elizabeth Newberry Sill. He taught school in Wadsworth and served as principal of Cuyahoga Falls High School.

Sill spent more than a decade in California at the University of California. He returned to Cuyahoga Falls in 1883 to devote more time to writing. Edward Rowland Sill is recognized as one of the nation's outstanding poets.

***

James A. Vaughn (1829-1889) was born in Mercer, Pennsylvania, and worked in Medina County, Ohio, clearing land and logging. At sixteen years of age he returned to Pennsylvania on foot and worked three years as a machinist apprentice.

While working in Davenport, Iowa, in 1853, Vaughn repaired a steam engine owned by A.C. and Henry Bill. They convinced Vaughn to move to Cuyahoga Falls and work for them.

In 1855, James married Mary N. Kelly. Vaughn joined Turner, Parks and Company as plant manager and machine designer in 1857, and in 1874, he became one of the principal owners of the company. Turner, Vaughn & Taylor Company eventually became Vaughn Machinery Company.

Machine shop of Turner, Vaughn & Taylor Company. Henry Newberry's mill is on the right. Turner, Parks and Company leased land and water rights from Newberry in the late 1800s.
Photo Courtesy of Taylor Memorial Library

Calvin W. Vaughn (1858-1929) was the son of James A. and Mary Kelly Vaughn. Calvin was born in Cuyahoga Falls, and graduated from Cuyahoga Falls High School. He married Lucy E. Treat of Tallmadge, Ohio, in 1882, and they had one son, Leland A. Vaughn.

Calvin W. took over his father's entire holdings at Turner, Vaughn & Taylor Company when James A. died. Calvin purchased all outstanding stock, and became sole owner of the company in 1895. In 1929 the company's name was changed to Vaughn Machinery Company.

The Vaughn Machinery Company – 1930s.
Photo Courtesy of Taylor Memorial Library

Leland A. Vaughn (1883-1975) was born in Cuyahoga Falls, the son of Calvin and Lucy E. Treat Vaughn. Leland graduated from Kenyon College and studied at Cornell University. He became the president of Turner, Vaughn & Taylor Company in 1929.

In 1915 he married Rebecca Johnson. They had sons, James A., Allan, and Gordon C., who became stockholders and directors in the Vaughn Machinery Company.

Leland Vaughn (center) discusses business with sons James A. (left) and Gordon C. Vaughn (right) of Vaughn Machinery Company.

Photo Courtesy of Taylor Memorial Library

* * *

George R. James (1854-1937) attended Cuyahoga Falls schools and apprenticed with Turner, Parks and Company as a machinist.

In 1881, Thomas Sidnell, D. F. Waltz and James organized the American Foundry & Machine Company. He married Sarah S. Upson in 1886. They moved to Bowling Green, Ohio, in 1889, but returned to the Cuyahoga Falls area by 1894.

A partnership was established with Albert R. Bates that resulted in the founding of the Falls Lumber Company. James also served as director at the Falls Bank, the First Central Savings & Trust, and the Falls Rubber Company. He was a trustee of the Falls Water Works when the water plant was built.

J. Max James (1895-1950) was born in Cuyahoga Falls, the son of George R. and Sarah Upson James. He attended Cuyahoga Falls schools, Buchtel College, Albion College, and Actual Business College. He married Elizabeth Mary Jones in 1917 and became president of Falls Lumber Company in 1938.

* * *

Thomas Francis Walsh (1858-1937) was born in Cuyahoga Falls, the son of William and Rosanna Carlin Walsh. Thomas attended Cuyahoga Falls schools and was admitted to the bar in 1883.

Walsh built the Akron & Cuyahoga Falls Rapid Transit Company, an electric railway that ran from Barberton to Kent. He built several other electric lines in New Jersey and Rhode Island. He married Sarah Isabelle Mahar in 1884.

Walsh developed the *Walsh Block* on the east side of Main Street in Akron, with brothers John and Cornelius, in the late 1890s. Thomas served as the president of Swinehart Tire & Rubber Company, as well as the director of several banks and businesses.

Cornelius M. Walsh (1864-1932) was born in Cuyahoga Falls, the son of William and Rosanna Carlin Walsh. He is remembered as a leading industrialist and philanthropist.

Cornelius began working for Howe & Company, a lumber mill, and eventually bought the firm. With brothers John and Thomas, he built the Walsh Building in Akron. He served as president of Walsh Lumber Company, Walsh Milling, Walsh Paper Company, Falls Hollow Staybolt Company, and Falls Savings & Trust Company (that later became part of the First National Bank of Akron).

Although all of Walsh's businesses were important, the company that had the greatest impact was Falls Hollow Staybolt. Those of us who have never heard of a "staybolt" need to know that staybolts were locomotive related.

Cornelius Walsh owned several companies including Walsh Lumber Company. His estate helped to fund Walsh Jesuit High School.
Photo Courtesy of Cuyahoga Falls Historical Society

A staybolt was used to hold in place the two steel sheets in the firebox of a steam locomotive. Bolts could range in size from 7/8th to 1 1/4th inch in diameter, and 6 to 24 inches in length. The firebox of a large locomotive could have as many as 3,000 staybolts.

Falls Hollow Staybolt made staybolts for locomotives worldwide. When the diesel locomotive came on the scene, around 1935, the need for staybolts began to decline. The last staybolt was produced at the plant in 1953.

* * *

Clair Clifford Loudon (1902-69) was born on a farm in Columbiana County, Ohio. He graduated from Hiram College and was a math teacher and coach at Cuyahoga Falls High School for a short time.

He married Dessie Shelton of Cuyahoga Falls in 1930. He worked in real estate and the retail coal business until the time of the *Great Depression*.

To provide income for his family, he began using his two coal trucks for over-the-road hauling, and in 1933, formed a partnership with Henry G. Bender. The men purchased the nearly defunct State-to-State Trucking Company, and by 1951, owned 250 trucks. Loudon served as executive vice-president of the successful Bender & Loudon Motor Freight Incorporated.

* * *

Clarence E. Motz (1897-1955) was born in Northampton Township, the son of William and Mary McCuskey Motz. Clarence graduated from the University of Akron and received his law degree in 1922. He married Maud Rudy in 1924.

He was a partner with the Motz, Morris, Wilson and Quine law firm. He was the president of Summit Publishing Company and the Cuyahoga Valley Savings & Loan Company. Clarence was always interested in politics, and was a delegate to the Democratic national conventions in 1940, 1944 and 1948.

* * *

Ray W. Heslop (1897-1953) was born in Marietta, Ohio, the son of Thomas A. and Lillie Abict Heslop. He married Kathryn Torbert in 1915 and came to the Akron area in 1916.

He immediately became involved in real estate and home construction. The Heslop Building & Realty Company is responsible for many of the residential developments in the Summit County area, including homes in Cuyahoga Falls, Goodyear Heights, Opportunity and Avondale Parks, and The Colony apartment complex.

Ray Heslop is credited for starting the first major post-war housing project in the area. Knowing that GIs would soon be coming home, Heslop acquired a large parcel of land on the west side of State Road. Said to be the largest housing development in the state of Ohio at the time, 549 homes and apartments were on the drawing board. Valued at $5,000,000, Heslop's development provided an opportunity for young married couples to own a home. On 23rd and 24th Streets, each house had two bedrooms on the first floor, a finished second floor bedroom, and a basement. On streets from 25th Street to Valley Vista Park, the second floor was left unfinished.

In 1949, Heslop began building another 293 houses on the east side of Cuyahoga Falls. Homes were modestly priced and young families flocked to these neighborhoods where tricycles lined the sidewalks. A three bedroom house was only $10,250 in 1949. The houses were new, the price was right, and Cuyahoga Falls was a great place to live.

Laundry flutters on a clothesline in the backyard of a Heslop home in 1949. The Heslop Company built houses for under $11,000 and created neighborhoods filled with baby carriages and swing sets. Young families flocked to the small new homes, causing Cuyahoga Falls City School District to build more schools to house the youngsters.

Photo Courtesy of Babette Robinson

* * *

James J. Lawson (1888-1962) was one of nine children born on a farm near Lawsonville, North Carolina.

His first formal education began when James was 23 years of age while working as a laborer on a Presbyterian grade school farm. The hard working Lawson later attended a Bible School in Tennessee, and went on to pay tuition at Hiram College by cutting hair and running the laundry concession.

He came to Akron in 1919 and worked in the rubber factories. Leaving the factory work behind, Lawson started a small dairy supply business in Cuyahoga Falls in 1922. He sold the business to a national firm in 1928, and for the next six years, operated a filling station in Kent, Ohio. Getting back into the dairy business, he developed the *gallon jug plan*, and began selling milk on a cash and carry basis in his own stores in 1939. Eventually he set up stores in nearly every neighborhood in Summit County.

James Lawson began bottling milk by the gallon in Cuyahoga Falls, and sold it in more than 100 retail stores in every neighborhood in the area by 1951. Lower milk prices and higher milk consumption resulted.
Photo Courtesy of Cuyahoga Falls Historical Society

* * *

Henry Newberry (1783-1854) was born in Windsor, Connecticut, and considered by historians to be one of the founding fathers of Cuyahoga Falls.

Henry's father, General Roger Newberry, a Revolutionary War soldier, purchased 1000 acres of land in Tallmadge Township in 1798.

Henry was educated at Yale College and married Elizabeth Strong in 1803. Upon his father's death in 1814, Henry inherited the undeveloped Ohio property. Newberry moved his family to the Western Reserve in 1824 and built a log cabin at Silver Lake.

Newberry owned all the land along the river south of Portage Street and east of the present Fourth Street. He built dams and mills, and engaged in farming, mining and manufacturing. In 1840 he built a large stone house at the east end of Broad Street. He served as the first postmaster of Cuyahoga Falls and held the offices of mayor and auditor of the growing village.

* * *

Joshua Stow (1762-1842) was Commissary Chief of Moses Cleaveland's surveying party in 1796. Stow traveled from Connecticut to the Western Reserve 13, times but never became a resident of the township that he purchased from the Connecticut Land Company.

On many of his trips he brought relatives and friends who settled in the area. He appointed William Wetmore of Middletown, Connecticut, as his land agent.

* * *

Looking at 1902

Step back to the year of 1902 and have a glimpse at the folks living in the Village of Cuyahoga Falls 100 years ago. How were the residents of this booming little town earning a living? What were the main occupations? Who owned property? Who were the village entrepreneurs?

We know there were no neurobiology professors, computer programmers, cell phone tower builders, jet airplane pilots, dot com company salespersons, power lawnmower repairmen, flashy car dealerships, rap music performers, cable television linemen, pizza delivery boys, nail salon operators or polymer scientists.

From the Village of Cuyahoga Falls section of THE BURCH DIRECTORY 1902, we select the following samples of residents and village businesses to share with the reader.

```
                          KEY
bds – boards          cor – corner          es – eastside
ext – extension       opp – opposite        res – residence
ss – south side       ns – north side       wks – works
ws – west side        wid – widow
(name in brackets) wife's name
```

Adams Allen R (Anna B) machinist, res ws Allen
Adams Mrs Etta R (wid James), res Reed
Adams Express Co, C A & C Depot
AKRON PEOPLE'S TELEPHONE CO, T L Stevens local mgr,
      Roethig Bldg
AKRON SAVINGS BANK (Cuyahoga Falls branch),
      J B Merrriman mgr, Front, both Phones
Allcock William (Ella), wks Nail Mill, res 426 Stone
Etling Della, dressmaker, res N Front
Evans Daniel, millworker, bds J S Hill
Evans Miles R (Elizabeth), marshal, res ws S Front
FALLS HOLLOW STAYBOLT CO (C M and J W Walsh),
      mfrs Hollow and solid staybolt iron, office and works
      Portage Street, both Phones (See index to ads)
FALLS LUMBER CO The, cor Broad and Water
Falls Rivet and Machinery Co The, J G Pope pres, H J
      Stambaugh Vice pres, Samuel Higgs sec, office and
      works cor Portage and R R
Falls Savings and Loan Assn, L W Loomis pres, E A Prior
      sec, J B Merriman treas, C T Grant atty, Savings
      Bank Bldg
Falvery Maurice, nurse Sanitarium, res same
Fenton Fred L (Elsie A), wiredrawer, res es S Second
Feucht Christ (Emily A), saloon N Front
Fisher Cornelius (Catherine), farmer, res ss Northampton ave
Fisher Emma, chambermaid Clifford Inn, bds same
Fisher James A (Augusta), hay dealer, res 124 S Fourth
Folger John, laborer, bds Water
Folger James, laborer, bds Water
Francisco Thos J (Lottie), cigar mfr N Front, res ws N Third
Freer Alice P, opr Am Tel & Tel Co, res ss Stow
Fretz Samuel K (Mary A), gardener, res ss Sackett
```
```

KELLER BRICK CO The, Fred W Keller pres, Wm F Keller
    sec and treas brick mfrs Cuyahoga Falls rd, both
    Phones
Keys Florence E, teacher res 135 S Newberry
Kidd Albion (Catherine), motorman, rms C E Harrington
King Prince, paperhanger, bds 212 S Fourth
Knapp Henry V (Marcia A), engineer Water Works, res Brick
Koonce Thaddeus B (Grace M), rubberworker, res Center
Kottka William E (Minna), wks Wire Mill, res ss Chestnut
Lantzer Solomon, wks Falls R & M Co, res Payne ave
Leader Frank (Emma), tanner, res es N Second
Lee Joseph G, clerk, res Main
Lewis Chester A, student, res N Front
Thompson, Charles H, wks Adams' Livery, rms same
Tifft George C (Nellie), meat market 110 N Front, res Allen
Tompkins Mrs Sarah, cook Hotel Warren, rms W F Curran
Treat Fred C (Stella L), draftsman, res e s N Second
Tremelin Mrs Elizabeth A (wid B B), res 315 Portage
Truax Francis E (Jessie L), oil dealer, res E Portage
Truax Lester, wks Wire Mill, res E Portage
Truman Carl R, clerk B & O Ry, bds 502 N Front
TURNER, VAUGHN & TAYLOR CO The, engineers, founders
    and machinists Broad st
Ulm Louis N (Minerva J), electrician, res School
Ulm Phillip (Catherine), res e s N Second
Ulmer Christian (A Mary), laborer, res 575 School
Welch Pearl, dressmaker, res w s S Third
Welsh John, clerk Walsh Milling Co, bds Miss S Marshall
West Karl H, wks Goodrich Co, res e s N Front
Westover Harry H (Jennie E), stonemason, res 513 N Second
Wetmore Fred G, clerk Loomis Hardware Co, res Stow Corner
White Harvey s (Birdie), wks Power House, res e s N Front
Wilcox, Lottie, bookkeeper, res S Newberry
Wilcox, Orlando (Zelia M), attorney, res S Newberry
Williams Alice, operator C U Tel Co, res J Cowen
Williams Emmet wks Rod Mill, res Brick
Willits B Frank (Abbie P), farmer, res 420 Stow
Wills Harry E (Clara L), grocer Loomis Block, res cor Front
    and Chestnut, People's Phone
Wilson Harry V (Mattie V), barber N Front, res S Front
Wilson Rev Welty J (Emma N), pastor M E Church, res w s
    S Fourth

* * *

The Falls Rivet & Machine Company, engineers, founders, and machinists were in business over 100 years ago. Office and works were located at the corner of Portage and the railroad tracks, according to the Burch Directory of 1902.

Photo Courtesy of Taylor Memorial Library

Consider This

Interesting facts compiled by the *Retired Educators Association of Minnesota* give us a glimpse of how life has changed since the early 1900s. The average life expectancy in the United States was 47 years. Only 14% of the homes had bathtubs, and 8% had telephones (a three-minute call from Denver to New York City cost $11.00).

The average wage in the U.S. was 22 cents per hour, with the average yearly income between $200-$400. Professionals such as accountants, dentists, veterinarians, and mechanical engineers made $2000-$5000 annually.

More than 95% of all births took place at home, and believe it or not, 90% of physicians had no college education. One in ten adults could not read or write and only 6% of all Americans graduated from high school.

* * *

Riding the Rails
(Special Thanks to John Phillips
for assisting with the following information)

Interurbans (electric rail cars) were owned and operated by the power companies. The transportation that these lines offered in the late 1800s through the early 1930s allowed the "residential sprawl" to develop throughout the Akron area. Houses were built in the remote areas of Kenmore, Barberton and Ellet, rather than in the inner city.

Two major financiers vied for the interurban business. John F. Seiberling, of Akron, had a successful electric line service running throughout the city. Competition arose when Thomas F. Walsh, of Cuyahoga Falls, decided to construct an interurban line that would run from Barberton to Kent. In 1892, in order to keep Walsh from having a monopoly on transportation to Cuyahoga Falls, Seiberling extended his trolley tracks up Howard Street in Akron, through North Hill to Chalker's Landing at Cuyahoga Falls Avenue.

Walsh, on the other hand, continued to move forward with his project and developed the "Akron-Cuyahoga Falls Rapid Transit Company". By 1894, the line ran down Furnace Street in Akron, across a 325-foot bridge over the Little Cuyahoga River, and across another bridge that spanned the larger Cuyahoga River. Because of the challenge of the rugged terrain, the train was dubbed the *Mountain Line.* By 1895, Walsh had developed an 18-mile transit service that ran from Barberton to Cuyahoga Falls, Silver Lake, and Kent. The interurban barns, and an area referred to as Silver Lake Junction, were located in Cuyahoga Falls in the general area of Hudson Drive and 2nd Street.

The infamous *Mountain Line* came to its demise as a result of a shocking and tragic accident. On June 11, 1918, the car was crossing the Glens Bridge at Prospect Street in Cuyahoga Falls when it crashed through the railing and fell 96 feet to the river below. Four people were killed. The city of Cuyahoga Falls insisted that the *Mountain Line* service be discontinued. By this time, The Northern Ohio Traction & Light Company owned the business. They had, in fact, built the large power plant on the Cuyahoga River to supply the electricity to operate the system. The last of the interurbans ran in Cuyahoga Falls in 1932.

Horse powered "herdics" were the first streetcars that appeared in Akron in the 1880s. Shortly thereafter, electricity was used to power the cars. Interurban transportation provided the much-needed means of travel within communities and eventually spread between cities in northeastern Ohio. But, by the 1920s, trolley and motor buses began replacing the electric rails that crisscrossed the country.

In addition to the interurbans, train service was available to shuttle products and people from city to city. As early as 1852, rail service was available in Summit County.

Unlike the coal-powered locomotives, a train referred to as *The Doodlebug* was a unique passenger vehicle. It was either gasoline or diesel driven and was a combination locomotive, coach, and baggage car.

One of Cuyahoga Falls worst disasters was the wreck of *The Doodlebug* on July 31, 1940. Thomas

Murtaugh, the engineer of the two car *Doodlebug*, failed to pull the train off to a side rail in order to let a 73-car freight train pass. Upon collision, the gasoline driven *Doodlebug* burst into flames and 43 passengers were killed. Murtaugh and two crewmembers jumped from the *Doodlebug* when they saw the 73-car freight train bearing down on them.

The Doodlebug was a diesel or gasoline driven passenger train that served as a locomotive, coach and baggage car. Tragically, on July 31, 1940, a two car Doodlebug traveling south through Cuyahoga Falls collided with a 73-car freight train. Forty-three passengers died.

Photo Courtesy of Pete Mellinger

Italians in Cuyahoga Falls
(*Special Thanks to Joe Maite*
for assisting with this information)

If you ask where the Italian families in the Akron area live, likely the response will be *North Hill.* And that is true. Numerous Italian families and businesses are located on the north side of the city. But were you aware that Cuyahoga Falls has a large Italian community?

Although there were people of Italian decent throughout the Falls, most settled in the Gorge area. The neighborhood is bordered on the north by Grant Street and on the south by Arcadia Avenue. Within that section are 9th, 10th, 11th, and Campbell Streets.

Looking back at the 30-year period of time from the 1930s through the 1950s, several names come to mind. There were the Caporaletti, Cortesi, Cioffi, Defago, Foti, Fiordi, Johnson, Lichi, Lang, Longhitano, Maite, Malorni, Marcello, Piglia, Polo, Prinzo, Ronca, Santos, (Scafidi, Scafido, & Scofido), and Vitali families. There were others of course, and it is always dangerous to list names for fear of missing some. However, we choose to give you a sampling of names in order to validate the presence of Italians in Cuyahoga Falls. Please remember as well, that there were numerous spellings of names of immigrants arriving in the United States.

If you could step back sixty years into the neighborhood, you would find that most folks had vegetable gardens, grape arbors, and fruit trees. Some families raised chickens and perhaps a goat or two could be found. It's possible that you could smell tomato sauce cooking and even hear the screeching of wanna-be accordion players.

It was in this neighborhood that the Italian American Citizens Club (IAC Club) was founded. In 1933, a group of interested individuals formed a committee to establish a social club for Italians in Cuyahoga Falls. Founding fathers included, Frank A. Lange, Nick Cardaralli, Tito Cortesi, Anthony Lichi, J. Selevesto, James Malorni, Louis Cioffi, Benny Johnson, Louis Caporaletti, and Anthony Fiordi, The club, at 1521 9th Street, continues to operate, nearly seventy years after its founding.

Several Cuyahoga Falls businesses were owned or operated by Italian Americans. Tommy's Café-Tom Bruno, City Poultry-Nunzi Fergoli & Michael LaCasella, The Star of Italy-Ralph Delisa, and Falls Stamping & Welding-Frank Lang. Tito Cortesi and Danny Marcello operated barbershops, and Jimmy Caetta had a fruit market on Front Street.

The Cozzoli, Fisher, Bulogna, Totaro, Manardi, and Scafidi families were in the grocery business. After World War II ended, there was a housing shortage as men returned from the battlefield. Louis and Pete Caporaletti built many homes for young families in Cuyahoga Falls. Ajax Construction Company, under the direction of Joe Scafido, Andy Malorni and Al Gauthier, was another Italian firm involved in the building trades. For several years Libert Bozzelli represented the "Italian Ward" in City Council.

Most first generation Italians were hard working energetic people who believed that the "new country" would provide them with an opportunity for a better life. They arrived in Akron looking for employment in one of the many factories in the blue-collar town. Children of these new Americans generally had a strong work ethic. Many of them went on to own or operate businesses and became, like their predecessors, productive members of society.

* * *

Silver Lake

We must consider the history of Silver Lake along with that of Cuyahoga Falls because of the close proximity and the many events and stories that cross political boundaries.

The Native American Indians most likely enjoyed the shimmering lakes and the availability of game in the woods nearby. It is believed that in the early 1800s, over 500 Indians lived in two camps in the area. Often called Mingos, they were a branch of the Seneca Nation. After the War of 1812 most Indians moved westward.

All historical records of Silver Lake discuss in great detail the Silver Lake Amusement Park built in 1874 by Ralph H. Lodge. It was indeed one of the most spectacular parks in the east. Lodge purchased the lake, along with 35 acres of land, and built a park that attracted visitors from as far away as Pittsburgh, Pennsylvania, and Columbus, Ohio.

A railroad brought up to 10,000 fun seekers daily to the grand playground. The park boasted roller-skating, bowling, swimming, and boating. There was a roller coaster, a Lake Launch, a 15,000 square foot dance floor, a baseball diamond, and the first airport in Summit County. In addition, the park was equally acclaimed for its live animal exhibits, including several black bears.

To the delight of swimmers, the beach was covered with sand shipped from Lake Erie. There was even a 444-foot long horse shed with 59 double stalls for the horse and buggy crowd.

When the railroad discontinued service to the Silver Lake area in 1912, the park was adversely affected. Heirs sold the property to real estate investors for $600,000 in 1918.

Today, the community of Silver Lake consists of 1,067 homes with a population of 3,019. The Charter type government, with a village council is presided over by

Mayor Warner Mendenhall. The Village maintains its own Police Department.

According to the Census 2000, the median household income was $70,875 for 1999, up 9.0% from 1989 figures. Only 2.8% were considered in the poverty range. Of those individuals 25 years of age or above, 50.6% had at least a Bachelor's Degree. The median home value was $190,700 up 24.2% from 1990 figures.

Silver Lake Village covers an area of 1½ square miles including Crystal and Silver Lakes. The Village Hall is located at 2961 Kent Road. Silver Lake Elementary School opened in 1919. The school merged with the Cuyahoga Falls City School District in 1965.

Silver Lake Amusement Park, built by Ralph Lodge in 1874, was one of the most popular recreational facilities in the east. The orchestra platform was suspended from the ceiling in the 15,000 square foot ballroom. Fun seekers arrived by horse and buggy, streetcar and railroad. Lodge died in 1907 and his heirs sold the property for residential development in 1918.

Photo Courtesy of the Cuyahoga Falls Historical Society

Northampton

Northampton Township's rugged terrain was most likely the reason for its slow development. It was part of Portage County in the early 1800s. In 1840 the state legislature mandated that Northampton and fifteen other townships would become the new Summit County.

Population of Northampton Township at that time was less than 1,000 hardy souls. It was unrefined territory and few individuals were willing to risk living miles from *civilization.*

Surveyors identified Northampton as Town 3, Range 11. It was the 11th range of townships west of the Pennsylvania border (55 miles) and the 3rd town north of the 41st parallel.

The Cuyahoga River was recognized as the boundary between the eastern and western Indian Tribes. Many groups, including the Mingo, Ottawa, Seneca and Delaware, identified the valley as neutral territory.

Records indicate that the first brave settlers to invade Northampton Township were Simeon Prior, a former soldier in the Revolutionary War, his wife Katherine Wright Prior, and their ten children.

These hardy folks traveled from Massachusetts by way of Lake Ontario, the Niagara River, Lake Erie, and finally on foot to Northampton Township. They purchased 400 acres and were quickly immersed into the pioneer lifestyle. Northampton supposedly got its name from a town near Prior's Massachusetts residence.

Names found in old records include: Nathaniel Hardy Sr., Able Vallen, David Parker, Rial MacArthur, David Norton, Daniel Turner, and Justice Remington,

Samuel King built a small hamlet known as Old Portage on the river. Later, around the time of the opening of the Ohio & Erie Canal, Birdsey Booth of Cuyahoga Falls built a warehouse at that location. Merchandise was received by canal boats daily, and farm products from northeast Ohio were shipped to markets in the east.

MacArthur's Corners, at what is now Portage Trail and State Road, was the location of the first small schoolhouse. Headmaster Justice Remington was the teacher in charge of a handful of community children in 1809. Eight one-room schoolhouses were built throughout the rural community over the next 100 years. In 1925 a central school was built that would house students, and the one-room buildings were phased out.

Religion played an important part in the life of the early settlers. The first formal church building was the Methodist Church, now the Northampton United Methodist Church, built in 1855 on land donated by Reese Jones.

Local residents manned the volunteer fire department that was first organized in 1945. A police department was started in 1961 with one patrol car and two policemen.

Northampton Township remained a relatively rural community for nearly two hundred years. Even as the cities of Akron and Cuyahoga Falls developed nearby, Northampton saw little growth. Large farms dotted the landscape, and it was a place one could go to enjoy nature. Blossom Music Center and the Cuyahoga Valley National Park located within the township provided recreational opportunities for those living in the Akron/Cleveland area.

But time changes things. And changes are happening in Northampton Township today. In 1986, Northampton Township, by way of merger, became Ward 8 of the City of Cuyahoga Falls. Ward 8 consists of approximately 18 square miles or 11,520 acres of land. Opportunities abound for commercial and residential development.

IV

Nature's Playground

*Cuyahoga River, Cuyahoga Valley
National Park, the Riverfront,
Parks and Recreation*

Lucky folks living in Cuyahoga Falls have a multitude of recreational activities from which to choose. Swimming, hiking, golfing, skiing, picnicking, river tours, and even skateboarding are just a few of the activities available for individuals of all ages. The presence of parks in Cuyahoga Falls is not a new concept. Actually, parks were located in the area when your great-grandfather was *wet behind the ears.*

Perhaps it was the beauty of the hills and valleys, the outcropping of rocks, and the enchantment of the water that first drew people to the Cuyahoga Falls area. Historians have documented fascinating information concerning some of the favorite playgrounds of yesteryear.

Parks of the Past

Silver Lake Park – As early as the mid-1800s, entrepreneurs identified Silver Lake as a possible resort spot. A bathhouse had been built on the east side of the lake in 1836, but the small steamboat and rental cottages built by Zira Buel in 1850, were designed to attract attendees.

Transportation in the 1800s was a challenge and getting to the park was a problem that could not be easily resolved. Buel's park was a failure.

In 1874 Ralph H. Lodge purchased the property from Horace Miller and then bought adjoining parcels of land He developed the 487 acres by building a resort and constructing a spur track from the C. A. & C railroad. The interurban rail lines built in 1895 brought thousands of fun seekers from Cuyahoga Falls and Akron, and Silver Lake Park's popularity spread throughout Ohio.

For its time, it was the most spectacular entertainment center around. It boasted the largest dance ballroom in the state, zoological gardens, several thrilling amusement park rides and up to 10,000 visitors a day. Although there were other amusement parks in the area, Silver Lake continued to operate long after Lodge's death in 1907. Family members sold the property for residential development in 1918.

Roseland Dance Hall at Riverview Park in the early 1900s was located in what is now the Gorge Metropolitan Park.
Photo Courtesy of the Cuyahoga Falls Historical Society

High Bridge Glens

Spectacular views of the falls from the outcroppings of the towering rocks attracted fun seekers of all ages. In 1878, L. W. Loomis and Harvey Parks developed High Bridge Glens Park south of Prospect Street. Front Street was often a sea of mud, but crowds flocked to the two-story dance hall, concessions and one of the country's first roller coasters.

A wonderful place to explore caves and climb about on the slippery ledges, the park was famous for its wooden Suspension Bridge, Fern Cave, Twin Rocks, Weeping Cliffs, and Observation Rock. Excursion trains including the C.A.&C. (Cleveland, Akron & Columbus Railroad) brought guests to High Bridge Glens.

Unfortunately, a number of tragedies occurred in the park, including the accident when the *Mountain Line* streetcar jumped the tracks and plunged to the river below.

For ten cents passengers could take the Silver Wave steamer launch, owned by Boys & Clarkson of Cuyahoga Falls, up the river a mile and a half to Snake's Den or Goose Egg Island.

Parks of 2002

Special Thanks to Superintendent Dick Pierson for assistance with the following information

One could say that every household in Cuyahoga Falls is within walking distance of a park. A city park, a school park, a metropolitan park or a national park. Ward 8, the Northampton area, is under development and residents will eventually have the same opportunities as residents in the older part of Cuyahoga Falls.

Residents of the city are fortunate to have political leaders who have advocated the development of quality recreational facilities for the citizens of the community. With talented leadership and financial support by the constituency, Cuyahoga Falls boasts one of the top sports and recreational programs in the state.

There was land set aside for park use in Cuyahoga Falls as early as the 1930s, but it was in the 1950s, when the Parks and Recreation Department was established, that a commitment for park development was confirmed. Roy Mann was the first Superintendent of Parks and Recreation, followed by Carl Fuest in 1954.

Don Hulick took over the helm from 1969-88, and since that date, Richard W. Pierson has served as Parks and Recreation Superintendent. It takes 25 full-time and over 100 seasonal employees to run the operation.

From 1960 through 1992 voters approved recreational *levies* that gave the financial backing necessary for a superior neighborhood park program. During this time period the School Board and the Park Board devised a plan that granted the city use of school sites. Along with a commitment on the part of the city for maintenance, a Recreation Program could easily be run with the facilities of school gymnasiums and fields.

In 1996 the city passed a 2% income tax. From those funds, 8% goes to the Cuyahoga Falls Parks & Recreation Department. Many of the recreational facilities are free to the public. Leisure activities that may include "user fees" generally take place at the Natatorium, Brookledge Golf Course, Water Works Family Aquatic Center, Downview Sports Center, and Quirk Cultural Center. In addition, several rental facilities are available for a variety of functions.

City of Cuyahoga Falls
Recreational Facilities and Acreage

Babb Run Bird Park/Wildlife Sanctuary – 25.1
Brookledge Golf Club – 120
Downview Sports Center – 22

Galt Park – 6 (Gift of Hugh Galt)
Harrington Field – 5.6
Indian Mountain Park – 4.5
Kennedy Park – 17
Keyser Park – 75.6
Linden Park – 3.5
Lions Park – 6.5 (Gift of Falls Lions Club)
Maintenance Headquarters – 7
Natatorium – 3
Oak Park – 5.1
Preston Park – 5
Quirk Cultural Center – 2.5
Riverfront Center – 10
River Front Park – 9
Ross Park – 8.6
Sedro Site - .5
Tot Lot - .3
Trails End Park – 8.9
Valley Vista Park – 11.3
Water Works Park & Aquatic Center – 151
Mud Brook – 40

Water Works Family Aquatic Center

Natatorium

There really isn't any reason that a kid from Cuyahoga Falls shouldn't know how to swim. With the YMCA, Water Works Family Aquatic Center, and the Natatorium, there are plenty of opportunities for swimming lessons and practice.

The Natatorium programming offers more than swimming lessons. But the major emphasis a few years ago was the year-round swimming facility.

Architect James J. Montalto designed the Natatorium with a unique and innovative vinyl-coated nylon roof that could be removed during warm months. Forced air furnaces were used in the winter to keep the 112 by 112-foot roof suspended. Beneath the roof was a 75' x 75' x 42' foot L-shaped swimming pool.

When the building opened in 1969 it was one of the first of its kind in the nation. The unique concept was recognized, and the Natatorium was the recipient of the 1969 "Outstanding Recreation and Park Facility Award".

One exciting event that took place in 1969, for the first time, was the use of the Natatorium by the Cuyahoga Falls High School graduation class as part of their *all-night graduation party*.

By 1976, it was necessary to consider replacing the nylon roof, and looking objectively at the energy costs associated with operating the facility. It was decided to put a permanent roof over the complex. This revision allowed for the addition of a sauna, whirlpool, elevated running track, and a fitness equipment and exercise room.

Two years later the use of the Natatorium had doubled. Informal fitness pass rates were $12.00 per month, with a special $7.00 rate for senior citizens. It was time to enlarge the facility. A men's locker room, two whirlpools, a new sauna and a 2,000 square foot fitness room were added.

Dedication of the third major addition was held in 1983. This phase included a new women's locker room, a concession area, a second running track, and six handball/racquetball courts. Over the next several years other improvements were made to the Natatorium.

Today, there are 13,000 names on the "membership" list and several thousand people use the "Nat" monthly. The Natatorium has always collected "user fees" guaranteeing that the facility is self-supporting. During the 2002 year, a thirty-day membership costs $25.00 for residents and $19.00 for senior residents. Annual unlimited usage passes were $275.00 and $209.00 respectively. Pool rentals are available for private parties at selected times. The Natatorium has 149 part-time and 3 full-time employees.

Programming includes, but is not limited to: group fitness classes, swimming, racquetball, weight training, cardio-fitness, Yoga/Tai Chi/Karate, and running/jogging.

In 2002, the city looks forward to the construction of a new Natatorium, or COMMUNITY RECREATION CENTER. Funds have been approved and the architectural team is finalizing the design.

Brookledge Golf Course and Downview Sports Center
(Some information taken from Parks & Recreation Report Notes)

Nearly 50 years ago, someone (probably a golfer) thought it would be a great idea if Brookledge Golf Course became a city owned golf course. It was owned by Don Walker and adjoined Galt Park.

Nothing much happened until 1974. Through the sale of bonds, and a matching $220,000 grant from the

Ohio Department of Natural Resources, the city was able to purchase the golf course. The 55 acres at 1667 Bailey Road was renamed Cuyahoga Falls Front Nine.

Renovations were started and the course was to open Memorial Day 1975. Mayor Robert Quirk was to hit the first ball off the seventh tee. The rental of a house on the property was offered to park supervisor Mark Johnson, and the city spent $150.00 on advertisements. It is said that the weather was exceptionally nice that year, and the golfers began arriving in mid-March, even though much work on the course was yet to be done.

Don Arnold owned 50 acres of land adjacent to the Cuyahoga Falls Front Nine. Plans began forming to acquire Arnold's property, as well as other smaller parcels nearby, so that an 18-hole course could become a reality. Eventually, approximately 80 acres was purchased.

In 1983, golf rates were increased to $3.75 for nine holes, and $5.25 for eighteen, Monday through Friday. Weekend rates were $4.00 and $5.50 respectively. A season pass was $185.00.

In 1986, the city hired golf course architect Arthur Hills of Toledo, Ohio, to develop plans for the new nine-hole course. Cavanaugh Building Corporation was hired to do the work. Montalto Architects were hired to design a new clubhouse. With the help of the fire department the old barn on the property was razed.

It was determined that not enough water could be pumped for irrigation of the course. Tests showed that about 50 gallons a minute could be pumped, but 700 gallons a minute was needed. Water lines were installed and the plan was to use city water.

Arthur Hills was hired again in 1989 to redesign the original nine holes at the course. The renovation budget was $400,000. Total income for the course that year was $246,478, up from $106,852 for 1980.

The course at 1621 E. Bailey Road is now called Brookledge Golf Club. The 2002 rates are weekday $12.00 for nine holes, $21.00 for eighteen. Weekend rates are $14.50 and $27.00 respectively.

City owned property at 1617 E. Bailey Road is called **Downview Sports Center**. Downview features 32 driving range tees, an 18-hole miniature golf course, batting cages, and the recently opened skatepark.

Perhaps a future major league baseball player may be training in one of the batting cages in Cuyahoga Falls.

School Parks

The Parks and Recreation Department has a working relationship with school districts that include the following school facilities: Bolich, Sill, Schnee, DeWitt, Falls High School, Lincoln, Newberry, Preston, Price,

Richardson, Roberts, as well as the Woodridge Elementary, High, and Middle Schools.

* * *

Gorge Metropolitan Park

The creation of Metropolitan Parks in Summit County began in 1921 when residents of Boston Township petitioned a probate judge for property. In 1926, the first of many generous gifts of land was received. What we have today is quite spectacular.

Presently, there are 7,000 acres of land, including a 27-mile Bike & Hike Trail, Seiberling Naturealm, and several large conservation areas in the Metropolitan Parks system. A Board of Parks Commissioners oversees 80 full time and numerous seasonal workers.

We are fortunate to have a beautiful Metropolitan Park here in Cuyahoga Falls. Visitors to the park come to see the rock formations and to hike the wooded trails. Often we forget how fortunate we are to have the Gorge in our own backyard.

The Gorge probably was a result of glacial activity. When glacial debris blocked the former route of the Cuyahoga River, the water found a new course. Geologists tell us that the riverbed is made of shale, and the ledges on either side are made of Sharon Conglomerate.

In the area of Gorge Metro Park was a park called Riverview Park. It operated from the early 1900s to the 1930s. Northern Ohio Traction & Light Company (later known as Ohio Edison Company) donated the 144 acres of land to the Metro Parks in the 1930s.

Visitors to the park enjoy hiking, ice skating, fishing, and picnicking.

TRAILS:

Glens (for a gentle hike) – 1.8 miles
Gorge (for a steep hike) – 1.8 miles
Mary Campbell Cave (for a gentle hike) – .6 miles
High Bridge (for a moderate hike) – 3.2 miles

Gorge Metropolitan Park provides visitors with trails for hiking, picnic areas and an abundance of beautiful scenery.

Fishing the Cuyahoga River

Do you remember when our "crooked river" was not as clean as it is today? Some of us can even remember when the river supposedly *caught fire*. Over the years, society has become more concerned with pollution and environmental health. The fact cannot be denied that there are toxins in the river that are a danger to fish *and humans*. Fortunately, regulations have been developed to monitor what mankind is doing to natural resources.

Advisories are published to inform the public of dangerous situations.

I have seen the youth cool themselves during the hot sticky days of summer by jumping into the Cuyahoga River. I have also seen folks fishing in waterways.

Do they eat the fish? Would you eat the fish?

The Ohio Department of Health publishes a FISH CONSUMPTION ADVISORY for the Cuyahoga River. From the advisory: *While most Ohio sport fish are of high quality, low levels of chemicals like polychlorinated biphenyl's (PCB's), mercury, and lead have been found in some fish from certain waters. To ensure the continued good health of Ohioans, the Ohio Department of Health offers an advisory for how often these fish can be safely eaten.*

These are the only species with advisories in the Cuyahoga River. Other types of fish are not covered by this advisory.

BULLHEAD – 1 meal per 2 months
COMMON CARP – 1 meal per month
LARGEMOUTH BASS – 1 meal per month
WHITE SUCKER – 1 meal per week (under 11")
1 meal per month (over 11")

Ohio EPA – Division of Surface Water
(Information from Fact Sheet and RAP)

- The Cuyahoga River is about 100 miles long and drains a watershed of 813 square miles. Although the watershed is less than 3% of Ohio's land area, it supports over 15% of the state's population.

- The Cuyahoga is one of only two rivers in the world that flows both south and north.

- In 1795 the Treaty of Greenville designated the Cuyahoga River as the western boundary of the United States.

- In 1832 the Ohio & Erie Canal opened for business as the nation's first inland waterway. The Canal was abandoned after extensive damage from the Great Flood of 1913.

- The Cuyahoga River watershed is home to 252 species of animals that are considered to be endangered, threatened, or of special interest. Seventy species of fish have now been collected in the river that was once considered *dead*.

Concerns about the cleanliness of the Cuyahoga River do not stop youngsters from fishing or playing in the cool water on hot summer days.

RAP *(Cuyahoga River Remedial Action Plan)* was established in the late 1990s subsequent to an agreement between the United States and Canada to clean up the Great Lakes. The Cuyahoga River was identified as one of 43 tributaries that would fall within the goals of the plan.

* * *

Cuyahoga Valley National Park

The spectacular 33,000 acres along 22 miles of the Cuyahoga River between Cleveland and Akron have been preserved for future generations. Approximately 3.5 million visitors annually take advantage of hiking, skiing, camping, picnicking, riding the historic steam train, visiting antique shops, buying fresh produce at local farms, and participating in other opportunities in the park.

It is estimated that man has occupied the Cuyahoga Valley for nearly 12,000 years. Historians believe that during that period of time prehistoric Indians, explorers, Native American Indians, trappers, traders, and settlers have inhabited the hills and fertile valley. The crooked river that flows through the territory has added commercial as well as aesthetic value to the region.

In the early 1900s it was recognized that this incredible valley should be protected. Akron Metropolitan Parks 1925 "Omstead Report" recommended that the entire valley be preserved in its entirety.

Hayward H. Kendall bequeathed 500 acres of land in 1929 to the State of Ohio for a park to be named in honor of his mother, Virginia. In 1940 an additional 800 acres of land was added to Virginia Kendall State Park.

Over the next several decades other parcels of land were acquired; the Boy Scouts and Girl Scouts of America, the Civilian Conservation Corps, Brandywine and Boston Mills Ski Resorts, and Blossom Music Center,

In 1956 Jonathan Hale's farm was bequeathed to the Western Reserve Historical Society. In 1970 joint effort was made by the Akron and Cleveland Metropolitan Park Districts for a $5 million matching money grant for preservation of the Valley.

Former Congressman John Seiberling actively took the lead in getting legislation passed to create a national park in northeastern Ohio. Finally, in 1974, President Gerald Ford, signed a bill authorizing 28,000 acres of land to become Ohio's first national recreation area. The *Cuyahoga Valley National Recreation Area* was established and the job of acquiring additional land and recreational opportunities was at hand.

The Ohio & Erie Canal Towpath trail of crushed limestone was dedicated in 1993. Up to 1.6 million people hike, bike and jog the meandering path through the valley. It is estimated that the park is one of the 15 most-visited of the 379 national recreational facilities. In 2000 the park became the *Cuyahoga Valley National Park.*

Eighteen square miles was added to the city of Cuyahoga Falls with the annexation of Northampton Township in 1986. Six thousand acres of the property lies within the Cuyahoga Valley.

* * *

Blossom Music Center

A bit of sharp cheddar cheese, a few crackers, fresh fruit, a blanket or lawn chairs, and a bottle of your favorite wine are the only necessities you'll need to bring. The Cleveland Orchestra will provide the entertainment at the beautifully designed Blossom Music Center.

Blossom Music Center is one of the finest performing arts facilities in the country. It is owned by the Musical Arts Association, the non-profit parent organization of The Cleveland Orchestra and Severance Hall. The House of Blues Concerts, Inc. of Los Angeles operates the facility. The name was chosen to honor the members of the Dudley S. Blossom Family, who have been major supporters of The Cleveland Orchestra for nearly a century.

In 1966 the Association selected 800 acres in Northampton Township, now the City of Cuyahoga Falls, on which to build the outdoor theater. Pietro Belluschi served as architectural advisor and the Cleveland firm of Shafer, Flynn and Van Dijk designed the complex. Christopher Jaffe did the preliminary acoustic design and Heinrich Keilholtz, a German acoustical engineer, designed the acoustical shell for the pavilion.

Music lovers settle in for an evening's entertainment at Blossom Music Center on West Steels Corners Road in Cuyahoga Falls. The sprawling complex serves as the summer home for the Cleveland Orchestra.

Photo Courtesy of Bill Katzenmeyer

Only 150 acres of the property have been developed. The rolling hills and acres of forest serve as a buffer between the Center and neighbors in the Steels Corners Road area. The grassy seating area is approximately four acres and can accommodate up to 13,500 people. The fan-shaped area and design of the pavilion allows for an unobstructed view of the stage. The covered pavilion seats 5,281 guests and boasts a 3,500 square foot stage.

Blossom Music Center features picnic areas, several gardens, a restaurant, an art gallery, a gift shop, and exquisite artistic sculptures throughout the park-like setting. In addition to serving as a summer home for The Cleveland Orchestra, contemporary rock, pop, and country entertainers perform on stage. When non-orchestra events are scheduled, there are restrictions at the gate concerning alcoholic beverages and other items.

The popular recreational facility, nestled among the hills, attracts spectators from the entire northeastern portion of the state.

Porthouse Theatre

Porthouse Theatre, adjacent to Blossom Music Center, is owned and operated by Kent State University. Performances include Broadway musicals, opera and drama. The summer stock theatre is open June through August.

* * *

V

Organizing for a Purpose

*Civic Organizations, Becoming a City,
Fraternal Groups,* Clubs, *the Arts,
Public Housing*

Man - A Social Creature

Mankind has always gathered together in groups for the purpose of accomplishing mutual goals. Whether it is to protect from enemies, form a body of governing members, build a highway, or to share common interests, individuals seem to benefit from being part of a group.

73

Committing oneself to an organization means working to support the mission of the group, sharing ideas with other members and working together.

Members of civic and governmental organizations often belong to the group through appointment or employment, whereas members of organizations, based upon common interests, receive satisfaction by way of association.

Mayors of Cuyahoga Falls

1837	Henry Newberry	1890-93	Sammuel Higgs
1838	Charles W. Wetmore	1894-99	D.F. Felmly
1839	Hosea Paul	1900-02	C.N. Russel
1840-43	Charles W. Wetmore	1903-04	E.M. Young
1844-45	Birdseye Booth	1905-08	Charles A. Davis
1846	Hosea Paul	1909-11	C.N. Russel
1847-48	Oliver B. Beebe	1912-21	W.H. Taylor
1849-52	Charles W. Wetmore	1922-23	George Herdman
1868	William A. Hanford	1924-27	Charles Gray
1869	Richard Blood	1928-33	George Porter
1870-71	C.P. Humphrey	1934-43	J.W. Haines
1872-73	Joshua L'Hommidieu	1944-49	Joseph W. Harding
1874-75	Horace B. Camp	1950-51	George A. Anderson
1876-77	George W. Rice	1952-53	Harding A. Wichert
1878-79	John I. Jones	1954-55	Elmer Wolf
1880-81	W.A. Hanford	1956-61	Emmet R. Wolfe
1882-83	J.C. Castle	1962-65	David Sanders
1884	A.B. Curtis	1966-68	Delbert Ackerman
1885	Sammuel Higgs	1968-69	Bruce Thomas
1886	Thomas H. Walsh	1970-73	William Coleman
1887-89	John I. Jones	1974-85	Robert J. Quirk
		1986-present	Don Robart

Cuyahoga Falls Fire Department

They may have been called "the bucket brigade" or the Hook and Ladder Company back in 1837 when Cuyahoga Falls was a village. You can bet that when there was a fire, the men came running from all directions, because of course, there was no fire station. Volunteers manned the buckets and did their best to douse the flames. Remember too, that most structures were made of timber, heated with fireplaces and lit with candles or oil lamps. A slight mistake and fire could quickly engulf a building or barn.

Uniforms, that is, a hat, frock and belt were purchased for the firemen in 1838. As the village population grew, so did the need for more fire fighters. Thomas Carney was the chief in 1888 responsible for directing two captains and twenty call men (all volunteers).

Fire Chiefs

1888-1889 Thomas Carney
1889-1902 William Clarkson
1902-1905 Irvin Loomis
1905-1910 Russell Post
1910-1912 Irvin Loomis
1912-1915 Frank Bethel
1915-1938 Myron Harrington, Sr.

1938-1959 Louis Seiler
1959-1975 Myron Harrington, Jr.
1975-1981 Elmer Brown
1981-1991 Wayne Bowen
1991-1999 R. Robert Leonard
1999- present Mark Snyder

In 1927 the Department was made up of a few paid firemen and several volunteers. Finally, in 1932, all members were paid. In the early 1900s the Fire Department was located in the basement of City Hall, located at Broad Boulevard and Front Street. In 1927, they moved to Front Street in what is known as Station #1

A long way from the Hook and Ladder days, the Fire Department of Cuyahoga Falls in the year 2002 includes; licensed paramedics, fire prevention programs, a Dive Team, a Rope Rescue & Extrication program, and citizen training classes in Basic Cardiac Life Support (C.P.R.). The Department takes care of hazardous materials handling (HAZMAT) and also has a Technical

Rescue Operation Team (TROT).

Today, there are 88 firemen, 2 Deputy Chiefs and 3 Fire Marshals in the Department.

* * *

Keepers of the Peace
Cuyahoga Falls Police Department
*(Special Thanks to Lt. Jack Davis
for assisting with this information)*

We feel secure in our communities when we know there are individuals that have assumed the responsibility of peacekeepers. They oversee the operation 24 hours a day, 365 days a year. We depend on them when emergencies arise and sleep well at night knowing they are on duty.

Cuyahoga Falls ventured into law enforcement in 1836 using the town marshal system. Sherman Peck was the first marshal, and he depended on volunteers to assist in the performance of duties. In the old western movies, the marshal is portrayed as a tough character that rids the town of unsavory characters. Certainly, the job of a marshal could be a dangerous one. But in Cuyahoga Falls, only one marshal was killed in the line of duty. Marshal Ira Goldwood died while trying to stop a run away horse on Front Street in 1906.

The last marshal to serve the city was William Sanderson who served from 1916-1922. Cuyahoga Falls made the transition from town marshal to a full fledge police department in 1922. The first Chief of Police was Russell Duffy who served from 1922-1946. In 1938 the department boasted a 10-man police force.

Chief Donald Brown led the department from 1964-1979. One of the many changes that came about during that period of time was the hiring of female police officers. The first four women police officers were hired in 1973. These women were hired to perform the same tasks as their male counterparts, but were paid $200 less a month.

The fourth chief in the history of the department was Chief Gene Fawley who served from 1979-1982. Charles Elum followed Fawley. Elum was chief from 1982-1986 when the City of Cuyahoga Falls merged with Northampton Township. This merger added ten police officers from the township to the force in Cuyahoga Falls.

Donald Smith became the next chief and served as the department leader from 1986-1999. The seventh Chief of Police was Louis Dirker Jr. who served from 1999-2001. By this time the police force had grown to 93 members, including 10 permanent community-policing officers.

Chief Gordon L. Tomlinson assumed leadership in 2001. Under his direction are; 2 Captains, 5 Lieutenants, 12 Sergeants, 75 Patrolmen and Patrolwomen, 3 Community Service Officers, 1 Auxiliary Services Manager, 15 Dispatchers, 1 Office Manager, 1 Chief's Secretary, 8 Records Employees, and 4 Youth Services Employees. A total of 128 individuals help to make Cuyahoga Falls a safe place to live and work.

* * *

Cuyahoga Falls Chamber of Commerce

At the annual meeting of the Falls Civic Association in 1926, a fifteen-member committee was appointed to organize a Chamber of Commerce. The first meeting was held at the City Hall that November. A membership campaign for the Cuyahoga Falls Chamber of Commerce, CFCC was held in January 1927.

Officers elected were: C.E. Motz, President; W.H. Richardson, First Vice-president; A.E. Ranney, Second Vice-president; D.D. Burgan, Secretary; Russell Frey, Treasurer.

In 1941 the Cuyahoga Falls Merchants and Manufactures' Association was formed, with goals similar to those established by the Chamber of Commerce in

1927. By 1950 that group officially changed its name to Cuyahoga Falls Chamber of Commerce.

Over the years the organization has been actively involved in local projects and issues facing the community. At one time the Cuyahoga Falls group was closely affiliated with the Akron Regional Development Board, ARDB. In 1986 the CFCC separated itself from the ARDB and established an office on Oakwood Drive.

Today, the Cuyahoga Falls Chamber of Commerce, under the leadership of Laura Petrella, Executive Director, is located at 2020 Front Street. Officers for 2002 are: Jeff Kline, President; Janet Roberts, First Vice-president; Dave LaRue, Second Vice-president; Jill Hanna, Treasurer; Angela Acello, Secretary. Current membership exceeds 300.

* * *

Robert J. Quirk Cultural Center

Adult coordinated activities take place at the Quirk Cultural Center. Named in honor of the former mayor of the city, who served the public from 1974-85, the facility is a meeting place for seniors.

Programs for senior citizens began in the 1960s. Activities were coordinated by volunteers from the Jaycees, Kiwanis Auxiliary, Veterans of Foreign Wars and the Rotary Club.

The Quirk Cultural Center is located in the former Grant School, which operated as a public school from 1930-1983. The building was closed due to declining school enrollment.

The building was leased to the Cuyahoga Falls Parks and Recreation Department. Remodeling took place so that the facility could be rented for dinners, wedding receptions and parties. The "Craft Shoppe" serves as an outlet for handcrafted items, and an active program for senior adults is ongoing at the Quirk Center. Activities include a travel club, dancing, crafts, bingo, and AARP #455. In 1996 the Quirk Center celebrated its 10th anniversary.

* * *

Clubs and Organizations Of Cuyahoga Falls in 2002
(from PARKS & RECREATION BOOKLET)

AARP Chapter #455
Akron Aquarium
  Society
Akron Camera Club
Akron Mineral Society
Alliance for the
  Mentally Ill
American Association
  of University
  Women
American Legion
  Charles
  Faust Post #281
American Sewing
  Guild
Ancient Order of
  Hibernians
Angel Wings
  Foundation
Antic, Inc.
  Comm.Theatre
Aquatic Club
Boy Scouts of America
Chair Caners
Country Place Support
  Group
CF Amateur Baseball
CF Aquatic Club/
  Water Works
CF Breakfast Optimist
  Club

CF Camping Club
CF Chamber of
  Commerce
CF Community Band
CF Community Chorus
CF Eagles
CF Eagles Auxiliary
CF General Hospital
  Community Board
CF General Hospital
  Guild
CF Good Neighbors
CF High School
  Student Council
CF Historical Society
CF Light Artillery

CF Little Black Tigers
  Cheerleaders
CF Little League
  North Baseball
CF Little League
  South Baseball
CF Masonic Temple
CF Moose Lodge
CF PTA Council
CF Schools
  ABLE-GED
CF Schools Alumni
  Foundation
CF Senior Travel Club

CF Shrine Club
CF Stamp Club
CF Woman's Club
CF Y/Nat Swim Club
Cuyahoga Valley
  Archaeological Soc
Cuyahoga Valley Art
  Center
Cuyahoga Valley
  Civitan
Cuyahoga Valley
  Youth Ballet
Democratic Women's
  Study Club
Eastern Star
Emotions Anonymous
Evening Optimist Club
Fair Housing Service
Falls Cancer Club
Falls Sil-O-Ettes
Falls Soccer Club
Families Anonymous
Family History
  Genealogical
  Research
Family Solutions
Fraternal Order
  of Eagles # 2207
Fraternal Order
  of Police # 49
F.O.P.A. #31

Fraternal Order of Police Auxiliary
Free & Accepted Masons Lodge #768
Free Spirit Cloggers
Friendship Club
Gertrude Sandford Doll Club
Girl Scouts
Goodtime Cloggers
Greater Akron Model "T" Ford Club
Hampton-Falls AARP #5038
Hill & Vale Garden Club
Humane Society of Akron
Info Line, Inc.

Instrumental Music Patrons
Jaycees and Jayteens
Kiwanis Club of Central CF
Knights of Columbus
Ladies Cemetery Association
League of Women Voters
Lions Club
M.A.D.D.
M.U.M. Mothers
Marine Corps League

Chesty Puller detachment
Memorial Day Comm.
Men's Garden Clubs of America
Mother's of Preschoolers
Mother's of Twins
Mount Akra Masonic Lodge #680
Myasthenia Gravis Foundation
Northampton Grange
Northampton Historical Society
Ohio Genealogical Soc
Oktoberfest
Old Portage Masonic Temple
Order of Eastern Star Falls Chapter
Order of Eastern Star #245
Paradise Social Club
Pet Guards
Porthouse Theatre
Pride Alumni Band
Rotary Club
Safety Town
Senior Strollers
Shrine Club
Sidelines of N.E. Ohio
Sierra Club
Silver Lake Historical

Society
Skyscraper Club of Cleveland
Soroptimist International
Sorosis Club
Soup's On at St. John's
Summit Lapidary Club
Swing Machine Band
Taylor Memorial Public Library
Technocracy, Inc.
Tiger Paws & Maws
TOPS #551, #300, # 978
Toastmasters #190
USS LaGrange Star Trek
United Daughter's of the Confederacy
Veteran's of Foreign Wars Ralph Huff Post
Veteran's of Foreign Wars Appleman Post #3294
Wa-Hoo's Square Dance Club
Walleye Association of CF
Walsh Jesuit Mothers
Widows & Widowers
Women's Democratic Study Club

* * *

Riverfront Centre Association

The Riverfront Centre Association promotes the Riverfront Centre District of Cuyahoga Falls. The organization's purpose is to advance the commercial, cultural, historical, community, and civic interests of its members and the public. Association officers for 2002 are: Doug Moore, President; Stacey Mathieu, Vice President; Lynda Tisch, Secretary; Don Dieterich, Treasurer.

Riverfront Centre is located in the historic downtown district adjacent to the Cuyahoga River. A pedestrian mall provides a scenic area for riverfront events amidst the shops, galleries, restaurants, hotel, offices, city services, and other businesses.

Portage Trail Village

You may recognize the large circular apartment building at 45 Cathedral Lane. Rex Humbard and the Cathedral of Tomorrow organization built it in the late 1960s. The purpose was to provide safe housing for those individuals who were down on their luck.

Portage Trail Village was built in the late 1960s by the Cathedral of Tomorrow to provide safe housing for those in need. Today, the 202-apartment complex is owned by National Church Residences.

The apartment building was sold in 1985 to National Church Residences (NCR) headquartered in Columbus, Ohio. The Rev. John R. Glenn founded NCR in 1961. The organization owns or manages 194 affordable senior housing facilities in the United States and Puerto Rico. Over 14,000 residents live in NCR housing.

Portage Trail Village was previously known as Cathedral Apartments. It is presently part of HUD, the United States Department of Housing and Urban Development. Jo Stanovcak manages the 202 apartments in Portage Trail Village.

* * *

The Cuyahoga Valley Art Center

In 1934 a small group of ladies met to found *The Arts & Crafts Club*. Original members were Virginia Hudson Clarke, Hallie Soleleather, Mrs. Arion Shaffer, Mrs. Joe Reager, and Mrs. N. G. Rongone.

By 1936 the club needed more space and moved to the Apollo Building on the corner of Front Street and Portage Trail. The entire country was suffering from the ravages of the Great Depression, and public schools deleted art classes from the curriculum.

With the support of the Falls Board of Trade, community leaders Laura Vaughn and I. Schoner, as well as School Superintendent Gilbert Roberts, a new mission was established for the club.

The name of the organization was changed to *Cuyahoga Falls Art Institute*. Goals were established that would provide art appreciation, through classes and exhibitions, for students as well as adults.

A move to the Plum Building on Portage Trail in 1939 provided more opportunities for the community. The first floor served as a gallery and workshops, while the second floor was leased to help defray operating expenses.

Mrs. H. M. Hagalbarger owned the building, and the M. O'Neil Company donated a piano. Now the Institute could offer classes in art, piano and dance.

Without a building of its own the Institute moved and changed names several times in the 1940s. At the Schoner Building it was called the *Art and Study League.* In 1945 the name was changed to the *Falls Civic Art Center,* and in 1946 it became *The Falls Art Center,* and moved to North Front Street.

In 1959 the group moved to the second floor of 1886 Front Street, and renamed itself *The Cuyahoga Valley Art Center* (CVAC), Patsy Sigler, Joe Ferriot, Larry Quackenbush, Marc Moon and other artists quickly established new goals for the organization.

The Women's Auxiliary of the CVAC was organized to provide financial aid, conduct fundraisers, promote activities, serve as volunteers, identify and support talented students, and to recruit new members.

Under the leadership of its first president, Patsy Sigler, The Women's Auxiliary of the CVAC seemed to be the catalyst that was needed to provide stability to the art center. In 1987, with the aid of the Women's Auxiliary, *The Cuyahoga Valley Art Center* purchased a permanent location at 2131 Front Street.

The permanent home includes 3,000 square feet of main gallery and classroom space on multiple levels. Over the years students have participated in drawing, composition, watercolor, acrylics, casein and oil painting, pottery, photography, enameling, etching, collage, basket weaving, piano, voice, dance, and drama.

In addition to those previously mentioned, some of the regional and renown artists who have been involved from the time of *The Arts & Crafts Club* through *The Cuyahoga Valley Art Center* of today include: Dino Massaroni, Tony Cross, Carrie Lewis, Jack Mulhollen, Jack Richard, Barbara Krans Jenkins, Charlotte Martin, Cathy Welner, Don Getz, Richard Cuckler, Jean Demer, Sandra Dennison, David Everson, Jeanne Hromco, Tom Jones, Jack Liberman, Beth Lindenberger, Marjorie

Lutes, Robert Putka, Judith Salamon, Mary Sanders, Judith Carducci, Peggy Wertheim, Joseph Fettingis, Peggy Strohmenger, and Hal Scroggy.

A gathering place for professionals and aspiring artists, The Cuyahoga Valley Art Center on Front Street began as an arts & crafts club in 1934. Pictured first row left to right Harriet Elson, Ann Kah, Jane Slivka. Second row Nicki Lanci, Mary Sanders, Joe Grace, Sam Hickman. Back row Tony Cross, volunteer Dice Moledor, Tom Jones, Managing Director & artist Linda Nye, Jack Mulhollen, John Bender, Hal Scroggy, and Coletta Bartlett.

* * *

Taylor Memorial Library

Can you imagine paying a "subscription fee" to borrow books from the library? That's the way it was in Cuyahoga Falls in 1883. If you paid the fee, only then could you borrow books to read.

Mrs. Margaretta Taylor, wife of industrialist William A. Taylor, felt that the citizens of the city should have a proper library. Mr. Taylor was a partner in Turner, Vaughn & Taylor Company, later known as Vaughn Machinery Company. And the Taylors were wealthy enough, and influential enough, to lay the foundation for the Taylor Memorial Library that is located on 3rd Street today.

In 1907 Mrs. Taylor bequeathed $15,000 for the land and a library building. Plus, another $3,000 was donated for the purchase of library resources. The William A. and Margaretta Taylor Memorial Association, a non-profit foundation, was created for the purpose of operating the library.

First library built in Cuyahoga Falls in 1912 on 2nd Street. Margaretta Taylor bequeathed $15,000 in her will for the construction.
Postcard Picture Courtesy of Pete Mellinger

A red brick library building at 2101 2nd Street opened its doors to the public in 1912. An addition to the facility was built in 1955 to meet the needs of the growing community.

Hoping to provide additional services, a branch library was opened and operated at Sill Jr. High School from 1959-70. However, by the mid 1960s, it was obvious that the small red brick building on 2nd Street was no longer able to house the library's growing inventory.

In 1970, after extensive political debate, a new library was built at 2015 3rd Street. A 99-year lease between the City of Cuyahoga Falls and the Taylor Memorial Association was established.

The Library Board of Trustees continues to be responsible for the operation of the library. Friends of the Library, founded in 1970, and numerous community volunteers work to support the library.

Over the years many local residents have generously donated to Taylor Memorial Library. The library received its first phonograph record collection, valued at $5,000, from Verne M. Robinette Jr. in 1954.

Businessman and long time resident, Frank W. Orth, contributed four bound volumes of the *Falls Reporter*, a local newspaper that was published for several decades beginning in 1870.

In 1980 the seldom-used Music Room was converted to the Local History Room. Rooms or spaces within the library often bear the names of donors. In 1978 Carl Graefe left $400,000 in a trust fund. His wife, Mary Anson Graefe, left $200,000 to the library at the time of her death in 1983.

The Chambers Room is named in honor of Harry and Margaret Chambers, and the Sutliff Room recognizes the contribution of Ray C. Sutliff. The computer room bears the name of benefactor, William H. Barth. Numerous works of art have been commissioned or donated by local artists.

Taylor Memorial Library continues to serve the community in a variety of ways. Circulation of library materials in the year 2002 exceeds 50,000 items per month.

There are two *Time Capsules* buried in the front yard of the library. A one hundred year time capsule was buried by the Cuyahoga Falls American Revolution Bicentennial Committee in 1976. It will be opened in 2076.

The second capsule was buried by the Cuyahoga Falls Chamber of Commerce in 1987, and it is scheduled to be opened in 2037. Wouldn't you love to see the reaction of those who will have the privilege of looking back in time?

Taylor Memorial Library 2002

* * *

Sunrise
Assisted Living

Cuyahoga Falls Sunrise Assisted Living facility is one of 225 Sunrise homes that provide care for seniors. Founders, Terry and Paul Klaassen, opened their first facility in 1981, striving to change the way society cares for the aged. The home for 68 individuals at 1500 State Road opened in 2000.

Terry and Paul Klaassen opened their first Sunrise community in 1981, with a mission to provide a better quality of life for seniors. Twenty-some years later there are 225 Sunrise homes, providing housing and care for nearly 16,000 senior adults.

In 2000, a residential facility was opened in Cuyahoga Falls at 1500 State Road that can provide assisted living for up to 68 individuals. Unlike the more institutional settings of traditional long-term care facilities, Sunrise residents experience the warmth and charm of a home-like environment.

Sunrise's commitment to quality of life includes private or companion suites, concierge service, outdoor gardens, fresh flowers throughout the residence, and a variety of social opportunities and educational programs.

There are approximately 50 employees. Don Poteet is the Executive Director and Rebecca Linton-Maruna serves as the Director of Community Relations.

* * *

Cuyahoga Falls Historical Society

In 1979 a group of historically minded individuals got together to discuss forming a society dedicated to preservation of Cuyahoga Falls history. After all, the city was nearly 170 years old, and little had been done to formally gather information concerning the development and growth of the community.

The steering committee and early members included William Barth, Connie Ankney, John Bender, Virginia Bloetscher, Paul Hillegas, Ione Hoffman, Connie Jenkins, Nina Perkins, Margery Smith, Ray Sutliff, and John Wafer. The non-profit group was incorporated in 1985, and Elizabeth Cross was named museum curator.

GOALS OF THE CUYAHOGA FALLS HISTORICAL SOCIETY
1. Collect and preserve historic records, documents and articles.
2. Organize and catalog the same in order to provide their accessibility to the public.
3. Engage in and/or support special studies and research related to the history of Cuyahoga Falls.
4. Explore sources of funding.

The Cuyahoga Falls Historical Society has worked diligently organizing and cataloging thousands of *pieces of history*. Volunteers staff the museum, answer visitor's questions and give tours to schoolchildren.

For some time the Quirk Cultural Center provided space for the museum. Recently, the museum has been housed in a building on Hudson Drive. The organization is in need of a permanent location where the history of

Cuyahoga Falls can be collected, preserved, and available for future generations.

* * *

Cuyahoga Falls General Hospital

Having a baby? Your neighbor broke his leg while repairing the roof? Your son has a skin rash that won't go away? Where do you go? Today, of course you can see a doctor, go to the hospital, or even stop at an emergency medical center. But years ago, it was not quite as simple.

Folks were fortunate if they had a doctor living nearby. Not all communities had physicians, and two hundred years ago, medical procedures were generally done at home or in the doctor's office. Medical instruments were crude, antibiotics were unheard of, and some doctors had never attended medical school.

Records indicate that around 1834, Chester W. Rice, M.D., began attending to health concerns of the residents of Cuyahoga Falls. Other members of the Summit County Medical Society who were from the Cuyahoga Falls area in the 1800s were Dr. William P. Cushman, Dr. John Davis, and Dr. John Strong Newberry.

In 1894, the first Cuyahoga Falls medical institution, Fair Oaks Villa Sanitarium, was opened. It was housed in the old Newberry Mansion. Later that facility became Fallsview Psychiatric Hospital.

In 1943, four osteopathic physicians opened Green Cross Hospital on the east side of Akron. Osteopathic medical schools trained doctors to evaluate the whole person. Andrew Taylor Still, M.D., was the 19th century Missouri physician who initiated the idea. Along with using every scientific advance available, physicians were also trained in the area of manipulative therapy. Based upon anatomical and physiological theory, physicians diagnosed and treated problems related to the muscles, bones and joints.

Green Cross Hospital soon outgrew its 34-bed facility. In 1954 a new hospital was built in Cuyahoga Falls. Additions to the facility have included a Professional Staff Office Building, a psychiatric unit and an Ambulatory Care Center.

In 1978 the hospital's name was changed to Cuyahoga Falls General Hospital. In 1995, the hospital joined the Northeast Ohio Health Network, which includes Akron General Medical Center, Barberton Citizens Hospital, Children's Hospital Medical Center of Akron, Medina General Hospital, and Robinson Memorial Hospital in Ravenna.

In 2001 Cuyahoga Falls General Hospital joined the Summa Health System. There are currently 257 beds, and the medical staff has grown from 190 to 300 in the past seven years. Of the medical staff, 30% are Primary Care Physicians. Jim Chromik serves as President and C.O.O. (Chief Operating Officer) of the facility.

Cuyahoga Falls General Hospital was founded as an osteopathic hospital, in 1943, by four doctors who opened a 34-bed facility in Akron.

Organizing for a Purpose

All-American Soap Box Derby
*(Special Thanks to Jeff Iula, General Manager
of the All-American Soap Box Derby, for assisting
with the following information)*

If we live in Summit County, it's in our blood. We grew up with the All-American Soap Box Derby and have attended the races at Derby Downs for as long as we can remember.

Local legend Billy Ford, of Cuyahoga Falls, the Suburban Champion with his family in 1970. The All-American Soap Box Derby originated in Dayton, Ohio, in 1934 and moved to Akron the next year. The Derby Downs racetrack was built in 1935 with the help of local officials and the WPA.
Photo Courtesy of the All-American Soap Box Derby

Racing is open to youngsters from 9 through 16 years of age. There are three racing divisions in most competitions. The Stock division is designed to give the first-time builder a learning experience. The Super Stock Car division is more advanced. By the time the boy or girl reaches the Masters division, the derby car has a very sleek look.

The Derby Downs racetrack in Akron is a 954-foot downhill run. Local champions from across the nation and throughout the world come to Akron during the summer to compete for scholarships and merchandise. During that week special programs are arranged for derby champs and their families.

Cuyahoga Falls was the site selected to host the North Summit Soap Box Derby Race for the first time in 2001. The 2002 race was also held in Cuyahoga Falls. Terry Anaszewicz, president of the North Summit Race, was assisted by numerous volunteers and local groups. The race was held on 13th Street and was typical of the races held some 40 years ago. Traffic was rerouted and bails of straw lined the roadway. Over 1,000 people cheered-on the racecar drivers.

Although Cuyahoga Falls has never had an All-American Soap Box Derby winner, several kids from the area have competed in the national races. Names that we recall are Eugene "Red" Miller 1947, Tom Beham 1969, Billy Ford 1970. Ryan McFall of Cuyahoga Falls was the only 3-time Akron local male champion.

When soap box racing first began it was a *boys only event*. Eventually, girls got in on the action. Today, many champions who participate in the All-American are female contestants from around the nation. Cuyahoga Falls has been represented by the following female champions: Shannon Gill, 2nd place in the 1988 All-American; Kelly Dughi, 8th in the 1993 All-American, and 1998 Rally Champ.

First annual North Summit Soap Box Derby racetrack on 13th Street in 2001. Champions qualified to compete in the All-American Soap Box Derby held in Akron, Ohio.
Photo Courtesy of All-American Soap Box Derby

* * *

Cuyahoga Falls Radio Club

There are many service, hobby and special interest clubs and organizations in Cuyahoga Falls. One organization that serves as a hobby for its 120 members, and also provides service for the community, is Cuyahoga Falls Amateur Radio Club.

These HAM operators come from every walk of life. They are all ages, sexes, income levels, and nationalities. There are more than 2,000 Amateur Radio Clubs nationwide. Although radio amateurs get involved in the hobby for many reasons, they all have a common basic knowledge of radio technology and have passed tests to receive a license.

There are three classes of Amateur Radio licenses. Each class requires passing a written examination dealing with radio regulations, operation and theory. Operators are permitted to operate in a series of bands throughout the radio spectrum from just above the AM broadcast band into the microwave region.

The Cuyahoga Falls club was founded in 1955 as an offshoot of the Buckeye Shortwave Radio Association in Akron. The Club's purpose at the time was to provide communications for Civil Defense Zone C (northern Summit County). The Federal Communications Commission (FCC) assigned call letters W8VPV to the club. The City of Cuyahoga Falls helped the group acquire some of its early equipment through federal matching funds for Civil Defense.

In 1961 the group began meeting at the Civil Defense building on Water Street. However, it was next to a power substation and that caused problems. They went to the American Legion Post on Front Street. In 1967 they began meeting at the United Electronics Institute on Orlen Avenue. Later they moved to Bishop Scout Center in Silver Lake, and finally in 2000, to Hope Homes in Stow. The Northampton City Hall will become the new home for the group sometime in 2002.

The club meets the 2nd and 4th Wednesdays of the month. A monthly newsletter, *Chattering Relay* keeps members informed of activities. Officers for 2001-2002 are: Mike Knapp, President; Bob McFadden, Vice President; Vince Scalia, Secretary; Ted Sarah, Treasurer; Dan Adkinson, Radio Officer; Cathy Ferry, Editor of *Chattering Relay*.

* * *

VI

Making a Buck in the Area

A Stroll Down Front Street
in 1948

Come with me for a stroll down Front Street in the days when traffic moved freely through the shopping area and the Riverfront Centre Mall was decades away.

Some of us were kids at the time and recall the many specialty shops and businesses that lined the street. There was **Lea Drug Store, Isaly's,** and **Miller's Restaurant** where many sport's banquets were held. **Leiter Hardware** was operated by father and sons, and not part of the conglomerate hardware stores of today. **Jone's Confectionery** served homemade ice cream and popcorn.

Customers line Front Street sidewalk waiting for a turn to purchase meat at the "Farm Boy Meats" market during the early 1940s.
Photo Courtesy of Cuyahoga Falls Historical Society

There was **Farm Boy Meats, Levinson's Department Store,** and **1st National Bank** (that since has been renamed **FirstMerit.**) **East Ohio Gas, Mair Jewelry,** The **M. O'Neil Company, Sord's Electric,** and **Kippy's Restaurant** were part of the scenery in 1948.

Lyn Bower and Harry Graham operated the **Falls Cigar Store.** Do you recall the **Fall's Pet Shop,** and how about the **Fall's Cycle Shop,** owned by Carl Fauley, located in the basement of the building? What about **Tommy's Café**, the **City Building**, **Standard Drug**, the **A & P Grocery Store**, **Fall's Theatre**, and **Fall's Savings & Loan**.

Many of the businesses were family owned and greeted regular customers by name. Plastic debit cards were not yet on the horizon, nor were cellular telephones, cable television, or e-Bay auctions. Life was much simpler in 1948.

A shave and a haircut at "Smoke" Summer's Barbershop under the First National Bank on Front Street.
Photo Courtesy of Taylor Memorial Library

As we look back we remember other sections of town where business was conducted. A strip of eateries and drive-in restaurants located on State Road included the **Canteen, Burrell's**, and the **B & B. Jimandy's** was opened in 1946 by Jim Tisci and Andy Silecchia. Do you remember the **Hungry I** on Portage Trail?

Several motels were found north of the city on Route 8 near **Ascot Park Racetrack**. The business district near Front Street and Hudson Drive was appropriately called the **Silver Lake Junction**. It had been the turn-around area for trolley cars and interurbans in the early 1900s.

Little shopping is done in the downtown Akron or Cleveland area in 2002. Most customers spend their money at major shopping malls or strip plazas.

Krieger's Health Foods Market

Have you purchased Ruby Red Florida grapefruit or perhaps your Christmas tree from the popular market at 615 Graham Road? Whether it is health food, fresh produce, or a turkey for your Thanksgiving table, quality and efficient service set Krieger's apart from other grocers.

If you have been in the area for many years, you probably bought produce from Mike Krieger's truck parked at the corner of State and Graham Roads (when Mike was still a teenager).

Ambitious Krieger had obtained a "huckster's license" from the Summit County Health Department when he was still in high school. At 16 years of age he was peddling produce door to door in Cuyahoga Falls, Stow, North Hill, and Silver Lake; and at 18 began selling out of the back end of his truck.

There were eight children in the Krieger family, and Mike fell somewhere in the middle of the large brood. Father was a German immigrant and Mike developed a hearty work ethic. When he was 13 years of age he worked as a caddie at Breathnach Golf Course, located in the Howe Road area, and started buying his own clothes.

However, selling produce out of the back end of his truck was not ideal, and eventually Krieger rented a small vacant house near the corner of Graham and State Roads, where the Double Play Miniature Golf Course is today. He ran an open-air market from that spot until the property was sold to the golf course.

When Mike was about 20 years old the opportunity came along to rent one-half acre of parking lot space next to Wootton's Tavern. He eventually purchased the property and over the years added to that small parcel.

Krieger's now own 11½ acres on Graham and Wyoga Lake Roads. The health foods market employs approximately 40 people. They have been in business for 38 years. The kid with the "huckster's license" done good!

Mike's partner in life and business is wife, Jean. They have three children; Christina, David and Susan. David operates Krieger's Fresh Market in Brimfield and Seven Grains Natural Market in Tallmadge. Christina and Susan have assumed much of the responsibility for running the Graham Road store.

Christina also owns a pet products wholesale business, and Susan works closely with her dad managing another of Mike's businesses - Krieger Communications.

Mike and Jean Krieger have numerous business interests. In 1989 they bought the tower on State Road left over from the Cathedral of Tomorrow days. It serves as a *communications platform.* They own many other parcels of real estate in the four county area and continue to work on developing those properties.

Krieger's Health Food Market on Graham Road. Other stores operated by the family include Krieger's Fresh Market in Brimfield and Seven Grains Natural Market in Tallmadge.

* * *

WBNX-Television

WBNX – TV, commonly known as WB55, broadcasts 24 hours daily providing programming from two networks: Warner Brothers Network and Fox Kids. WB55 started as an independent station in 1985, became the home of Fox Kids in 1994, and then became Cleveland's WB Network affiliate in 1997.

WBNX-TV is a commercial television station owned by Winston Broadcasting Network, Inc. The television station has been at its present location for 16 years. Lou Spangler serves as its president and general manager.

Although WB55 broadcasts to the entire Cleveland, Akron, and Canton, Ohio markets (the 15th largest television market in the United States), its studios are in

102

the heart of Cuyahoga Falls at 2690 State Road, behind the Cathedral Buffet & Banquet Center.

Active in community events throughout the entire viewing area, the WB55 event staff, with the WB's mascot, Michigan J. Frog, can be seen at area games, fairs, concerts, theme parks, and festivals throughout the year. WB55 is a favorite with young adults and kids. WB55 has the largest "kids club" in Ohio, and ranks second in the nation with over 150,000 members.

* * *

The "Farmer's Market" in front of Falls Theater on Front Street was important during the lean years of 1931-1935.
Photo Courtesy of Taylor Memorial Library

The clock on the wall says 9:05, and already at this early hour, women and a few men, wait in line during the war years, for an opportunity to purchase meat at Farm Boy Meats on Front Street.

Photo Courtesy of Cuyahoga Falls Historical Society

* * *

Levinson's

Solomon Levinson was born in Lomza, Poland, in 1887. He came to the United States in 1900. Sol's first job was that of a "cleaner boy" in a wholesale clothing house in Pittsburgh, Pennsylvania, when he was 13 years of age. He worked from 8:00a.m. to 6:00p.m., Monday through Saturday for $3.00 a week.

As an adult he worked as a retail store manager in several stores in Ohio and Michigan. Finally, after the flood of 1913, he opened his own store in Pittsburgh, Pennsylvania. Suits could be purchased for $10.00, and a complementary shirt cost 50 cents. He married Sarah

Cohen in 1914 and came to Cuyahoga Falls, setting up business at Portage Trail and Front Street.

In 1933 he moved the store to its present location at 2231 Front Street. The general store stocked items needed *from cradle to grave.* Levinson's has been selling clothing, accessories, and supplies to police officers, fire fighters, postal workers, and other uniform-wearing customers for decades.

Sol Levinson retired in the mid 1970s, and his son Gus, took over the family business. Following in his father's footsteps, Gus watched the store grow. In 1985 Bill Burch became co-owner of Levinson's in Cuyahoga Falls as well as another Levinson's in Canton.

* * *

Central Instrument Company

On the north side of the street in the 700 block of Portage Trail sits a building that is sure to get your attention. Three artistic giant-size horns are perfectly silhouetted on the exterior west wall of the establishment. What else? Of course, it's a musical instrument company.

The 739 Portage Trail address was once a Lawson's store and later housed Shephard's Candy. Owner and president of Central Instrument Company, Inc., James Stahl, moved his business from Tallmadge to 739 Portage Trail in 1984.

Instruments, accessories, and music scores can be purchased. Talented instructors are available to give music lessons at Central Instrument. A major segment of Stahl's business involves the rental of instruments to school students.

He works closely with music departments of local schools and parents of children who borrow or rent beginner instruments. If the student is successful and intends to continue the study of music, parents often purchase rather than rent the instrument.

Central Instrument Company on Portage Trail serves young students through the rental of music instruments. The building had been occupied by Lawson's and Shepard's Candy stores before James Stahl took ownership.

Photo Courtesy of Jim Stahl

* * *

The Million Dollar Mile

From the 1960s until the late 1970s the *Million Dollar Mile* was located on Front Street in Cuyahoga Falls. The Riverfront Centre Mall was not yet built and traffic moved in both directions through *downtown.*

A brainchild of the automobile dealers, the *$1,000,000 Mile* was an advertising vehicle that encouraged prospective buyers to shop for cars in a concentrated area. Each dealership contributed to the fund that was used to jointly purchase advertisement in newspapers, radio and billboards.

What was the significance of a million dollars? A million dollars worth of automobiles were on display within the mile. If the same strategy were used for advertising today, it would have to read 500 million dollars. But in the sixties and seventies the cost of most new automobiles was under $8,000. Buyers were encouraged to shop the entire mile to find the exact vehicle that suited their needs.

You may recall **Morgo Lincoln** and **Falls Dodge.** There was **Albert Conn,** who sold **Plymouth** products, and Joe Conn, who had the **Conn Ford Dealership.** John Lambert purchased the property at 2904 Front Street from **C. M. Jones** that soon became **Lambert Buick-Pontiac-GMC.**

Wallace Oldsmobile was located on the strip. Do you recall **Lyle Chevrolet?** And how about **Clarke Hayne VW** as well as Haggarty VW? Tim Thomas of **Thomas Chrysler Plymouth** started helping his dad with the business in 1972. **Thompson Pontiac** was located on Front Street as was **Ackerman's Firestone Store.**

America's Safest Car, The Finest Automobile Buy, and *Symphonic Styling* were slogans found in automobile advertising on Front Street prior to the **Million Dollar Mile** era.

Conart Motors sold Plymouths and **Hirsch Motor Company** sold Packards in 1936. **Lyle Chevrolet Company** was located at 2252 Front Street as early as 1939.

C. M. Jones sold the modernistic looking Studebaker automobile in the mid-1940s. And in the early forties, **Ray L. Winkler,** at 707 Front Street, advertised Hudson automobiles for as little as $670. Folks shopping for a new Buick in 1941 found the starting price was only $915 at **Harry G. Newcomb's** place.

Lambert Buick-Pontiac-GMC and **Thomas Chrysler Plymouth** are still on Front Street, but most other dealerships have moved elsewhere.

107

Today, if you are shopping for an automobile, you may have to drive from one end of the city to the other end, to find what you want. **Cascade Audi**, owned by Don Primm is located at 4149 State Road. The **Clarke Automotive Group**, owned by Todd Clarke, who followed his dad Bob into the business, is located at 4100 State Road.

John Spitzer started the business, and now son Al Spitzer, owns the **Al Spitzer Ford** dealership at 3737 State Road. **Falls Dodge,** at 3457 State Road, is owned by Paul Hrnchar.

The **Marhofer Auto Family**, owned by Ron Marhofer is located at the southeast end of the city, at 1350 Main Street.

Thomas Chrysler Plymouth Jeep, and Lambert Buick Pontiac-GMC, are the only two new automobile dealerships on Front Street. Most other showrooms are located north of town.

* * *

Falls Music Center, Inc.

In 1948 brothers Frank and Raymond Zucco, who were professional musicians, set up a one room music store on Front Street in downtown Cuyahoga Falls.

Raymond ran the business while Frank continued working in the music department of the M. O'Neil Company, a retail business in Akron. Both men worked the busy evening hours at the store.

By 1952 the brothers expanded their instruments and accessories business to include print music and lessons. A move to 127 Portage Trail in 1956 with the purchase of nearby property expanded their floor space to 8,000 square feet.

Again, by the mid-1960s, the rapidly growing music trade required more space. Zucco's acquired 131 Portage Trail, the former Cuyahoga Falls City Club, increasing their showroom area to over 18,000 feet.

In 1998 a 10-year employee and longtime friend, Robert W. Gallagher, purchased the 50-year-old company. Falls Music Center is one of the oldest and largest retail businesses to remain in what was downtown Cuyahoga Falls. The small one room music store started in 1948 now employs 35 people and is a regional landmark for the sale of pianos and instruments.

* * *

Clifford-Shoemaker Funeral Home

In the time of sorrow it is important to have a reliable source to help make plans and carry out necessary procedures. Residents of Cuyahoga Falls have relied on the Clifford-Shoemaker Funeral Home for these services for nearly 50 years.

Bill Clifford began working for the McGowan Funeral Home a short time after he was discharged from military service in 1946. Clifford quickly learned the trade. Eleven years later the Weller Funeral Home on Front Street was available, and Clifford purchased the business and changed the name.

With a fine reputation, the funeral home grew and became a permanent part of the landscape on Front

Street. The name was changed again in 1989. Clifford's daughter, Marlene Shoemaker, and her husband Ken, manage the funeral home on a daily basis today.

* * *

Krieger Communication Tower

You've seen it. How could you miss the tall concrete tower located on State Road? From nearly every vantage point in north Akron and Cuyahoga Falls you can see it!

Left over from the Cathedral of Tomorrow Church days, the 494-foot tall structure looms over the area like an unwelcome intruder on the horizon.

Perhaps the reason it bothers us is because it looks unfinished. It is unfinished! The original plans called for a revolving restaurant, an observation deck and antennas meant to send the gospel worldwide. Unfortunately, the tower was never completed and stood unused for many years.

Mike Krieger of Krieger Communication and Krieger's Health Foods Market on Graham Road purchased the tower in 1989. When others could think of no way to use the tall structure, Mike envisioned the concrete base as a foundation for communication satellites. And he was right about the use of the tall cement eyesore. There are currently several tenants who rent space or "bands" on the tower.

Literally seen for miles, airplane pilots perhaps more than anyone else, can appreciate the structure. It is definitely an identifiable landmark for those airplanes flying in northeastern Ohio.

Tons of cement went into the construction of the open top tower that rises high above the street level. For those interested in the towers "specs" - 494 feet tall; Latitude 41°N; Longitude 81°W; AMSL: 1041 feet (base of the tower).

110

Krieger Communication Tower looms over the city like a relic from the past. Although the original plans were to make it into a theater, a revolving restaurant, and an observation deck, today, it serves as a tower for communication satellites.

* * *

MR. FUN'S COSTUMES & MAGIC EMPORIUM

You say you need a costume for the neighborhood Halloween party? A hairy gorilla, a salacious dancing girl, or a grave robbing ghoul? I know just the place! Mr. Fun Inc. at 3503 Wyoga Lake Road has 10,000 costumes from which to choose.

Carol and Al Pocock were schoolteachers that got involved in the school carnival business back in the late 1960s. They bought a *Fun Services* franchise, and began servicing schools with "Santa's Secret Shop" in the early 1970s. In 1975 they bought a building on Wyoga Lake Road. PTA (Parent Teacher Association) moms would come to the store to buy prizes for school events.

Adults as well as children began celebrating Halloween in the 1980s, changing the focus of the business for the Pococks. Having left their schoolteacher jobs, they ventured out on their own, minus the franchise support. They changed the name of the business to MR. FUN'S COSTUMES & MAGIC EMPORIUM.

They opened a store in Brooklyn (near Cleveland, Ohio) in 1981. A store was opened in Kent, Ohio, in 1990; it was eventually sold to a former employee. The Medina, Ohio, store opened in 1995 with additional costumes and magic show supplies.

Mr. Fun Inc. employs 15 people full-time and has 30-35 seasonal employees. The Pococks are far removed from the classroom, and are having lots of fun.

* * *

W. L. Tucker Supply Company

In 1915 Walter L. Tucker from Clarksville, Ohio, came into town and bought a wagon and a horse named Joe. Tucker purchased the Northend Coal Supply Company, and put Joe to work delivering the black bituminous stuff to the homes in Cuyahoga Falls. Northend was renamed W. L. Tucker Coal Supply Company.

Eventually motor driven trucks replaced Joe, and Walter built a railroad trestle and silos for the storage of materials at the 2nd Street address. As gas furnaces came onto the scene, it was necessary for the small company to diversify. Coal furnaces were on their way out, and the community was gradually switching to the newer, cleaner way of heating homes. It was necessary for Walter to make some changes. Today, Tucker is a major supplier of hard masonry building materials.

Walter Tucker, and his horse Joe, delivered coal to Cuyahoga Falls residents and businesses in 1915. Today, W. L. Tucker Supply Company employs 35 people and operates a fleet of trucks.

Photo Courtesy of W. L. Tucker Supply Company

Tucker's daughter Elizabeth, and Richard (Dick) L. Hurley, both 1939 graduates of Cuyahoga Falls High School, married and were immersed in the family business. When Dick, an Air Force pilot, returned from World War II in 1945, Walter built the young couple an apartment above the business office. Dick attended evening college at Akron University while delivering coal and sweeping floors at Tucker Supply.

Upon graduation from college, Dick eventually became managing director of the company. Keeping up with the times and the burgeoning construction of new houses, Tucker Supply provided contractors with building materials. "Coal" was dropped from the name since the company delivered the last coal in 1968.

Today, the Hurley's only child, Elizabeth (Marty) Hurley Cailor, serves as CEO, and son-in-law Robert Cailor, is president of the builders' supply company. Except for the changes made when Route 8 was built, W. L. Tucker Supply has remained at the same location for over 85 years. Walter and Joe's small operation has grown significantly, and now the company employs 35 individuals.

*** *** ***

Schwebel Baking Company
(Lawson Milk Company)

Founded in 1906 in the home of Joseph and Dora Schwebel of Campbell, Ohio, the baking company on Newberry Street has an interesting past.

Dora assumed leadership of the family operated business in 1928 after the death of Joseph. She was able to keep the company solvent even though the depression years were difficult. Under her direction the company moved to a new $100,000 facility in 1936.

Another plant was constructed in Youngstown in 1951, and in 1972 the Canton Distribution Center opened. Second and third generation Schwebels assumed positions in the company as business continued to grow.

In 1976 the Vienna Baking Company of McKeesport, Pennsylvania, was purchased, and finally in 1981 Schwebel bought Lawson Bakery of Cuyahoga Falls, Ohio. Today, in addition to the plant, there are three Bakery Outlet Stores in the Summit County area; one at 3670 State Road, another at 1031 Kenmore Boulevard, and a third at 344 Tallmadge Road.

A Columbus, Ohio, Distribution Center opened in 1983 and Schwebel began supplying bread to Epcot Center in Florida. In the 1980s and 1990s Schwebel acquired Millbrook Bread of Cleveland, Ohio; Kroger Bakery in Solon, Ohio; and Kaufman Bakery of Hebron, Ohio.

Bread, dinner rolls, buns and the like, come from this plant on Newberry Street. Formerly, the building housed Falls Rubber Company and the Lawson Milk Company. Schwebel Baking Company took over the building in 1981.

Contracts with Stouffer's and Pillsbury helped to earn the Schwebel family a spot in the *Family Business Hall of Fame.* Four generations have been involved since Dora baked that first loaf of bread in her kitchen nearly 100 years ago.

Folks who have been in the area for some time will remember when the brick building adjacent to the railroad tracks at Broad Boulevard was once called Falls Rubber Company. Later it became the Lawson Milk Company. James J. Lawson got into the milk business in the 1920s when route drivers delivered quart and pint bottles of milk directly to customers' homes. Lawson believed customers would be willing to give up home delivery in order to save a few pennies on a gallon of milk.

He was right. The new marketing approach changed forever the way milk reaches our kitchens.

Gallon jug packaging of milk was new to the country when James Lawson of Cuyahoga Falls introduced it in 1939. The concept quickly spread, reducing the price of milk in the new cash and carry convenience stores.
Photo Courtesy of Cuyahoga Falls Historical Society

Lawson knew that selling milk in gallon jugs rather than quarts and pints could reduce the overall price. The public liked the idea.

At first, folks came to the plant to purchase milk. Within a short time he established convenience stores throughout the city, where milk, bread and a few grocery products could be purchased. By the early 1950s there were over 100 Lawson's stores in Summit County. The gallon jug concept spread nationwide, and credit is given to James Lawson for the innovative marketing strategy.

Lawson Milk Company was sold to the Consolidated Foods Corporation in 1958, and to the Sara Lee Corporation in the early 1980s. Later the Dairy Mart Company controlled the operation, and eventually, baked goods replaced milk products. Since 1981, Schwebel Baking Company has operated the plant on Newberry Street.

* * *

McCready's Tire & Auto

If you have a serious automotive problem, McCready's on Hudson Drive is the place to go. The shop is a mainstay in major and minor repairs, electrical systems, brakes, tune-ups, and other labor intensive or customized work.

Owner, Harold McCready has worked on automobiles, trucks and race cars since he was a kid at Cuyahoga Falls High School. While in school, McCready had a job at the Standard Oil service station on Front Street. He eventually bought and operated that business from 1971-1983.

In 1978, Harold and his wife Diane, purchased the big old building at 2726 Hudson Drive in order to be able to do heavy mechanical work. Former owners of the structure had been; Hoffman Tire Company, U. S. Gasket & Shim, and R.C.A. Repair.

Historians tell us that at one time this general area was called the *Silver Lake Junction*. It was the *turn-around* for the Akron city streetcars and interurbans that ran from 1890 to 1932. There were crews quarters above the offices in what is now Rockne's Pub on Hudson Drive.

McCready left a couple of well paying jobs to be his own boss. He worked at Trump Plastics, and was a supervisor at Industrial Electronic Rubber in Twinsburg,

Ohio. This self-taught guru of the automobile has upgraded his training and the shop's equipment in order to stay up-to-date on today's electronic/computerized vehicles.

Harold McCready, long time employee Jeff Patterson, and Jeffrey McCready of McCready's Tire & Auto on Hudson Drive. The building is located in an area referred to as the *Silver Lake Junction*, a yard, barn and turn-around spot for Akron city streetcars and interurbans from 1890-1932.

Business owners know the value of good employees. Harold speaks highly of mechanic, Jeff Patterson, who was hired six months after McCready's opened. Willard Livingston, another loyal employee, has been with the business for over 20 years. Son Jeffrey McCready, an Akron Paramedic, works part-time for his dad. If bodywork is needed, referrals are made to son-in-law Jerry Shaw who operates a shop on 2nd Street.

McCready's quality work and honest business dealings keep customers coming back. A small advertisement in the telephone yellow pages, and word of mouth is enough to keep six employees busy 10-12 hours a day.

* * *

Construction of the Ohio Edison dam and power plant changed the Cuyahoga River water flow. The original waterfalls can no longer be seen.

Cuyahoga Falls changed from a sleepy little milling town in the 1800s to the second largest city in Summit County at the end of the 1900s. Looking south during the construction of the Sheraton Suites in 1989. Route 8 (expressway) upper left.

119

Newspapers of Cuyahoga Falls

I enjoy reading the newspaper. I especially enjoy reading about what is going on in my community. Residents of Cuyahoga Falls have been able to keep up on events through a weekly newspaper since 1833!

As we look back at the history of the newspaper in the city, there are brief periods of time that cannot be documented. Whether it is because there was not a publisher at the time, or the possibility that records have been lost, no one knows for sure. We will share with you, what we have found about the weekly local newspaper.

Records indicate that from 1833 to 1838 the title of the paper varied. It was either called the *Ohio Review* or the *Cuyahoga Falls Review.*

Beginning in 1840, the *American Eagle* was published. For several decades, beginning around 1870, the *Cuyahoga Falls REPORTER* kept residents informed.

Around 1928 the weekly newspaper was called the *FALLS News.* This is the same paper we now recognize as the *Cuyahoga Falls News-Press.* In the late 1960s the publisher began producing the *Hudson Hub* and the *Stow Sentry.*

There was another paper in Cuyahoga Falls in the 1960s and 1970s. *CITY Press* was published by W. L. Pierson and was considered a rival of the *FALLS News.*

Newspaper folks for the last 170 years have tried to make sure the community has had access to local information. Today, the *Record Publishing Company* publishes *the Cuyahoga Falls News-Press.* The local office is at 1619 Commerce Drive in Stow, Ohio. This firm also publishes the following weekly newspapers: *Aurora Advocate, Bedford Times-Register, The Gateway News, Hudson Hub-Times, Maple Heights Press, The News Leader, Stow Sentry, Tallmadge Express,* and *The Twinsburg Bulletin.*

The Ohio Historical Society has copies of a variety of the old Cuyahoga Falls newspapers. Taylor Memorial Library has copies of newspapers back to 1870 that are available upon request.

* * *

The Hidden Pearl

Does nostalgia ever sweep over you and bring back bits and pieces of the past? You remember the television show *Father Know Best*, and for some unknown reason you begin humming the musical tune "Somewhere Over The Rainbow". You recall the glitter of the rhinestone earrings your mother wore, and the everyday "housedresses" that your grandmother wore (instead of blue jeans).

There are seven antique shops in the Riverfront Centre Mall. **Silver Eagle**, the **Blue Moon**, **Time Zone**, **Falls Antiques & Collectibles**, **Signature Gifts**, **Oakwood Antiques**, and **The Hidden Pearl**.

Sea Houser, owner and operator of The Hidden Pearl, has been in business on the Mall since 1984. She has watched as six different proprietors have moved in and out on either side of her shop. When the Riverfront Centre Mall was created, it changed not only the vehicle traffic pattern, but it also changed the types of shops located on Front Street. Planners envisioned that the mall would be an attractive shopping area. Specialty shops, boutiques and small eateries would line the street. Special events would bring folks to the mall and shop owners would be pleasantly pleased with the amount of business generated.

The mall is certainly nicely designed, and weekend events throughout the summer do indeed bring many people to the area. But there are numerous vacant storefronts. Merchants are hoping the new festival site planned for construction in 2002-2003 will bring the shoppers back to the mall.

In Houser's shop, in addition to her smiling face and good humor, you will likely find Victorian through 1970's clothing, jewelry, hats, hatboxes, purses, doilies, textiles, glass, pottery, and much more.

Whether it's books, antiques, collectibles or special gifts, the shops at Riverfront Centre Mall offer what cannot be found at today's mega-malls. These shops are generally open during special events and offer the customer a step back in time.

Sea Houser, proprietor of THE HIDDEN PEARL in the Riverfront Centre Mall, stands among the vintage collectibles.

* * *

Reuther Mold & Manufacturing

Karl A. Reuther, following his sweetheart to the land of opportunity, immigrated from Germany in 1928. In the old country he had been a machinist apprentice, and the training served him well in finding work in the New World.

By 1950, Karl A. was ready to step out on his own. He founded Reuther Mold in Akron, Ohio, and a year later moved his young business to Cuyahoga Falls. In the

1970s, sixty percent of the factory production and most of the company's profit was tied to the automotive industry. Reuther made rubber injection and compression molds for gaskets, as well as, molds that formed the weather stripping for wing windows on automobiles.

Karl A. A. Reuther, company founder Karl A. Reuther, and Karl Reuther, II, inspect a piece of equipment at Reuther Mold & Manufacturing Company on Munroe Falls Avenue.
Photo Courtesy of Reuther Mold & Manufacturing

In 1972 Karl A. retired, and son Karl A. A. Reuther became president of the company. Having been trained as a mechanical engineer at the Massachusetts Institute of Technology, Reuther was well suited for the job.

A major change in the company came about when the Employee Stock Ownership Plan was instituted in 1987. Today, family members control seventy percent of the privately owned company, but 30 percent is employee owned. Two worker owners sit on the firm's Board of Directors.

The third generation Reuther moved into the driver's seat in 1994, when Karl A. Reuther, II replaced his father, Karl A. A. Reuther, as president and CEO of the company. Over the years the product line has grown and changed. Today, the company makes molds to produce parts for rubber track diaphragms, engine seals, respirators, gas masks, tennis balls, automotive engine mounts, electrical insulators, and components of rockets and missiles – as well as other items that Karl A. could not have possibly envisioned in 1928.

* * *

Alside

Alside is one of the top vinyl siding and window manufacturers in the United States. With 3,000 employees, company headquarters are located in Cuyahoga Falls. Sales reported for the year 2001 - $524 million.

Your grandfather probably painted his own house. Most likely, the weather took its toll on the paint job, and Gramps had to drag out the paint bucket and ladder every few years.

Today, thanks to Jerome Kaufman there are other options. While serving in World War II, Kaufman observed that paint bonded to the aluminum fuselages of airplanes. When he returned to Akron in 1945, he spent considerable time developing a new formula for paint and an undercoating that would stand 15 years of wear. He also designed and made equipment that produced aluminum siding for the building trades.

In 1947 he bought five acres of property on West Waterloo Road in Akron, Ohio, and went into business with his brother Manual and a group of investors. Donald L. Kaufman, brother of Jerome, joined the legal department of Alside in 1955. Before long, Alside became one of the largest users of sheet aluminum in the world.

The plant on Waterloo Road was gutted by fire in 1958, and for a short time the company leased property on Gilcrest Road. A new plant and a unique butterfly-shaped office building, acclaimed to be the only one of its type in the country, using aluminum both on the interior and exterior, was built in Northampton Township.

By 1961 Alside was listed on the New York Stock Exchange. In 1969, U. S. Steel purchased all of Alside's outstanding stock for 25 million dollars, and Alside was recognized as the leader in both the steel and aluminum siding industry.

During the 1970s the company entered the vinyl siding business. More plants and company-owned Supply Centers were opened nationwide, and the research department began to investigate other product lines.

Founder Jerome Kaufman retired in 1983 and Donald L. Kaufman became Chief Executive Officer. Texas financier William W. Winspear purchased Alside, for 148 million dollars, along with two other companies from U. S. Steel in 1984 to form Associated Materials Incorporated.

Today, Alside Inc. consists of seven manufacturing facilities and 89 distribution centers located across the United States. Vinyl products have replaced the aluminum and steel. A research and development facility is located in West Salem, Ohio. Within the company are three divisions specializing in fencing, garage doors and cabinetry for kitchen and bath.

Mike Caporale was appointed President and Chief Executive Officer of Alside in 2000. The company has international exposure and continues to explore new product lines. Jerome Kaufman's pursuit of baked enamel siding over fifty years ago, was the beginning of a billion-dollar industry.

* * *

VII

People In Our Lives

THOSE WHO HAVE MADE A DIFFERENCE IN THE WORLDWIDE COMMUNITY

Keith Haag
- Architect -

If you have been to see a production at the Porthouse Theatre or pulled your car into a spot at the Summit County parking deck, then architect Keith Haag has touched your life.

Nationally renowned in the field of architecture, calling Cuyahoga Falls home, Haag has significantly influenced the design and structure of hundreds of commercial and private buildings nationwide.

In this area, Haag homes are easily recognizable and are often compared to the contemporary designs of Frank Lloyd Wright. He has been the chief architect in many additions made to local church buildings.

He designed Stow's Town Hall, worked extensively with the Lawson Milk Company and Humbard's Cathedral of Tomorrow. He was a valued consultant to Tom Dillon, developer of the Sheraton Suites, in the preliminary conceptual design of the hotel. Haag was the architect for seven buildings on the Kent State University Campus. He designed the remodeling of the Ohio Building in Akron.

Keith graduated from Cuyahoga Falls High School in 1946. He received a four-year degree from Kent State University and went on to get a Bachelor of Architecture's degree from Western Reserve University in 1952.

Haag set up practice in an office on the second floor of Tucker Supply Company. In 1961 he purchased a derelict piece of property on Chestnut Boulevard from the city for owed back taxes of $1,650. It was necessary to build a bridge across the water to where Keith wanted to construct his new building. Many people doubted his success; however, the building is still in use today.

Keith married Eleanor Baker Lawson in 1961. Both had been previously married, and there were five children in the blended family. Haag had been the architect of the Eleanor and Richard Lawson house on Steels Corners Road. When Eleanor was widowed, and needed to have an addition built onto the house, she called Keith.

Buildings house, shelter and serve us in numerous ways. Many are functional in design and serve the purpose for which they were built. But some are unique and aesthetically satisfy our need to be surrounded by beauty. The next time you dine at the Sheraton Suites, cantilevered out over the water, remember Keith Haag, architect extraordinare.

* * *

William Leonard Haines
1897-1991
- Creator of Street-Address Directory -

Most all major cities have street-address directories that identify residents and occupants of buildings. One northeast Ohio directory company produces books for one-quarter of the United States. The directories that service many of the country's major cities are called *Haines Criss+Cross City & Suburban Directories.*

William Leonard Haines graduated from Cuyahoga Falls High School in 1916. He married Minota Thompson in 1917. They had four children; William Kendall Sr., Mary Elizabeth Haines McGeorge, Leonard W., and Nancy Jo Haines Brannick.

William attended Ohio State University for two years, and went on to become a Second Lieutenant in the United States Infantry. For approximately seven years he worked in the credit bureau industry in Florida.

In 1928, after returning to Ohio, Haines became the founder of *Stark Legal News,* and in 1932 he founded the *Haines Criss+Cross City & Suburban Directories* business. Today the Haines Company also owns *Americalist*, a direct marketing firm.

Sixty years after the founding of the company, William Kendall Haines, Sr. is Chairman of the Board, and William Kendall Haines, Jr. is president of the North Canton, Ohio company.

* * *

Harry E. and Robert G. Heath
- Community Leaders -

You say you know the Heath brothers? Not surprising! They have unbounding energy and personalities like radio's infamous "Click & Clack" brothers. Complimenting each other, sharing stories and laughs, and serving the city in a variety of ways, make the Heaths a popular commodity in the area.

They were born in Berkley, California, and served in the armed forces. They arrived in the North Hill section of Akron in 1946, and shared a double room at the YMCA.

Bob and Harry will tell you that they attended *Saturday-Nighter Dances*, met girls, got married, bought houses five doors apart in "Heslopville" on Anderson Road, and began raising their families.

Harry worked 42 years as a tool and dies maker, and now drives a limousine shuttling folks where they need to go. For the past 19 or so years, he has been part of a volunteer group who coordinates the Oktoberfest. Presently serving as General Chairman, Harry gives the committees credit for the success of the festival.

Harry served on the clock tower committee, he coached peewee football for 13 years, and has taught Sunday School at the Methodist Church. With a grin, he tells of taking up sports car racing after his fifth child was born; an activity that his wife called *shenanigans*.

Bob spent 42 years in the field of education. He was a school principal for 36 years in the Cuyahoga Falls City School District, and now serves on the School Board. He is a member of the Parks and Recreation Board, and actively assists Harry with the Oktoberfest. At least one day a week, and sometimes two, he drives for the American Red Cross.

In the mid-1970s the Heath brothers were involved with Little League Baseball. Bob felt sure that the 12 acres of land they were able to purchase for $18,000 in Northampton would someday be part of the city of Cuyahoga Falls. He was right.

Both men are part of the Cuyahoga Falls High School, *chain gang*, measuring and marking plays at the Tigers football games. These avid fans attend home and away games, and help to support the youth by selling 50/50 tickets at the basketball games.

Some 20 years ago they were asked to run the casino event at the all-night graduation party. They are still doing it, and still loving it!

Harry and Bob Heath have given their time, talent and enthusiastic support to the community. The city and its people have been extremely fortunate to have the Heath brothers call Cuyahoga Falls home.

* * *

Charles J. Boyd
1908-2001
- Dance Instructor -

Charlie Boyd shuffled and tapped his way into the hearts of students, audiences and Cuyahoga Falls residents for nearly a century.

Born in 1909, in a house on Tallmadge Road, the talented son of Matthew and Olive Boyd, charged a nickel for backyard performances as a child. Although his father was not impressed with Charlie's interest in dancing, it was Olive who transported the boy to and from dance lessons.

Graduating from Cuyahoga Falls High School in 1928, Boyd went to New York where he worked in nightclubs and continued to study dance. He enjoyed performing, and traveled throughout the United States and Europe.

Coming back to Cuyahoga Falls, he worked as a salesman for Gardner Shoes. In 1935, he rented a hall above the shoe store on Front Street and began giving dance lessons. In 1936 he opened the Charles Boyd School of Dance on Second Street.

For the next 60+ years Boyd taught thousands of couples, children and even grandparents to dance. Many of his students became successful in the field of entertainment or opened dance studios of their own.

Boyd belonged to Dance Masters of America and Ohio, Dance Educators of America, and the National Association of Dance & Affiliated Arts (N.A.D.A.A.). Even at the time of his death in 2001, Charlie was teaching dance part-time at St. John's Episcopal Church in Cuyahoga Falls, and St. Bernard's Catholic Church in Akron.

Because of his love of acquiring antiques, Mr. Boyd's house was filled with hundreds of collectible items at the time of his death. A portion was left to personal friend James Hay, and the remaining household contents were willed to the Cuyahoga Falls Historical Society.

Charles Boyd, a 1928 Cuyahoga Falls High School graduate, danced for audiences across the United States and Europe. He eventually returned to Cuyahoga Falls, where he taught dance lessons from 1935 to 2001.

Photo Courtesy of the Cuyahoga Falls Historical Society

* * *

Mayor Don L. Robart
- Mayor -

The longest serving Mayor in the history of Cuyahoga Falls moved from North Hill in Akron to a cape cod house on 12th street when he was seven years old. The young Don Robart considered the community a *new frontier*, and was soon enrolled in Lincoln Elementary School. He graduated from Cuyahoga Falls High School and began attending Kent State University.

During the Vietnam War era, Robart served for a short time in the military. Returning to Cuyahoga Falls, Don began a 20-year career with The Firestone Tire & Rubber Company, and attended college part-time.

In 1981 the Republican Party invited Robart to run for mayor. He was not successful against Mayor Bob Quirk, but Don had been bitten by the political bug, and aspired to pursue a political office.

In 1983 he was elected to City Council. Robart became Mayor of Cuyahoga Falls in 1985. He was reelected in 1989, 1993, 1997 and 2001.

During his tenure, the city tripled in geographic size due to the annexation by merger of Northampton Township.

* * *

Dr. William B. Rogers
- Pediatrician -

Bill Rogers was born in Dayton, Ohio in 1918, and moved to Akron, Ohio, as an infant. His dad got a job as a ticket agent at the Akron Union Train Depot. Bill graduated from North High School and was able to take the bus from his home on North Howard Street to Akron University to continue his education.

Even though he was an only child, the expense of medical school was more than his family could afford. About the time that Bill was ready to pursue his goal of becoming a doctor, John S. Knight, of the *Beacon Journal Publishing Company*, established the C. L. Knight Memorial/Scholarship Fund in memory of his father.

Pediatrician Dr. William B. Rogers treated thousands of children during his 50-year practice on 2nd Street in Cuyahoga Falls.

Rogers applied, and was granted the funds necessary to allow him to attend the University of Maryland, School of Medicine in Baltimore.

During his second year in school, World War II erupted, and all medical students were drafted into the military. The government allowed the students to finish their education before being assigned to active duty. Dr. Rogers was sent to Frankfort, Germany.

When Rogers returned to Akron, he completed a one-year internship at Akron City Hospital. At that point in his career, he decided that he wanted to specialize, and began a two-year program in pediatrics that took him to Akron Children's Hospital and Columbus, Ohio Children's Hospital.

Eventually Dr. Rogers bought a duplex in Cuyahoga Falls on 2nd Street. He lived upstairs with his family and practiced medicine on the first floor.

Dr. Rogers recalls that in the mid-1940s, during his last year of residency at Akron Children's Hospital, the Polio Epidemic began its march. He describes it as mass hysteria, and remembers that there were so many sick children that the gymnasium of the church next to the hospital had to be used as a hospital.

Another event is memorable to Dr. Rogers. With the discovery of penicillin, finally there was a treatment for meningitis. Up until that time, meningitis was generally fatal. However, because of the severe shortage of the newly discovered miracle drug, it was necessary to call Boston, Massachusetts, to request the needed medication.

Bill Rogers married June Thomas of Silver Lake, and they had four children; Paul, Robert, Lenora and John. Two of the sons followed their father into the medical field. Paul is a pediatrician in Baltimore, Maryland, and Robert is a child psychologist in the Akron area.

After June's death, Dr. Rogers married Rosaria Shullo, a long-time friend who at one time had been a receptionist in his office. For health reasons, Dr. Rogers stopped seeing patients in 1999.

We would guess that Dr. Rogers has treated thousands of children during his 50 years as a pediatrician. This kind and gentle man developed great rapport with youngsters when they visited his office.

At the doctor's office children received a coin for the gumball type machine that dispensed trinkets. Today, Rogers still carries trinkets in his pockets, and when he sees former patients at the Giant Eagle grocery store or other places about town, he cheerfully hands out trinkets – putting a smile on everyone's face!

* * *

Jack Richard
- Artist -

Energy and enthusiasm abounds as Jack Richard bustles about his studio located near the fountain on River Front Centre Mall. Well known in the immediate area, Richard is recognized as one of the nation's most prolific portrait artist.

His credentials include training and experience from the Chicago Professional School of Art, Kent State University, Akron University, and Ohio University. He has studied or worked with nationally prominent artists such as Robert Brackman, Aaron Bohrod, Ben Stahl, Herb Olsen, Charles Burchfield, and many others.

He is affiliated with Stevens Gross Studios, Cliff Eitel Studios, Manning Studios, Richard Krupp Studios, and Cinecraft Productions. Richards is a member of I.P.A. (International Platform Association).

Richard has been the subject of numerous articles in a variety of publications including; *Who's Who In American Art*; *Fifty American Artists*, Asahi Press, Kyoto, Japan; *Contemporary Personalities*, Italian International Publication; and *American Artists of Renown*.

Jack is most pleased to talk about the more than 4,000 students who have attended his art classes over the past 45 years. Several have gained important national reputations becoming portrait painters, landscape artists and gallery directors.

136

Richard has been commissioned to paint 300 portraits of famous people and celebrities including Arnold Palmer, Bing Crosby, Bob Hope, Nancy Lopez, and President John Kennedy.

A painting of former President George Bush was commissioned by the World Series of Golf and hangs in the Bush Museum and Library.

Richard once painted 1,500 watercolors in two years to illustrate a television program on Ohio history. He is talented in the area of restoration and conservation of art works. There are several murals in the Akron area as well as at other sites throughout Ohio featuring Jack's work.

The Jack Richard Studios is located at 2250 Front Street. The artist has been giving lessons, restoring paintings and painting the "rich and famous" for 45 years. Celebrities include President George Bush and golfer Chi Chi Rodrigues.

Gates McFadden
(Cheryl Gates McFadden)
- Actress -

Dr. Beverly Crusher of Star Trek (Gates McFadden) is a local gal who attended Crawford Elementary School. These days she spends her time on the stage in New York or California.

You may recognize her as the popular Dr. Beverly Crusher on *Star Trek: The Next Generation*. She is a Cuyahoga Falls/Silver Lake gal who has been extremely successful in the theater, television, and movies.

Daughter of Veronica and William McFadden, Cheryl Gates McFadden was born March 2, 1952. She attended Crawford Elementary School and Our Lady of the Elms High School. She went on to Brandeis University in Waltham, Massachusetts, known for its theater program, and then studied in Paris, France, under Jacques LeCoq.

Heading back to the United States, McFadden spent several years in New York City prior to landing the *Star Trek* role. She played in numerous theatrical productions, including *Cloud 9, Emerald City,* and *Matchmaker.* She directed and worked on choreography and puppet movement for Jim Henson's *The Muppets.* She was a faculty member at New York University and Brandeis University.

Television credits are too lengthy to list, but include; *The Crosby Show* (when she was known as Cheryl McFadden), *Marker* in 1995, *The Practice* in 2000, and *Desert Princess* in 2002.

She was featured on the cover of *TV Guide* in 1994. Movies include *Hunt for Red October* and *Taking Care of Business.* Cheryl's most long lasting role has been that of Dr. Beverly Crusher, born 2334 on the planet Luna, in the series *Star Trek: The Next Generation* that began in 1987.

She has become an icon to the "Trekkies" who adamantly keep *Star Trek* alive. McFadden, and her character, Dr. Beverly Crusher, can be found on numerous web sites. Dolls, autographed photographs, and collectible memorabilia from the show are available on the web.

McFadden is married to John Talbot, and has one son, James Cleveland. The family resides in California, and travels frequently to Silver Lake to visit Cheryl's parents. McFadden is currently acting, writing and directing.

* * *

Russell S. Colley
1898-1996
- Father of the Space Suit -

Russell S. Colley lived to be 98 years of age and invented numerous things that we take for granted today. Colley was born in Stoneham, Massachusetts, and attended the Wentworth Institute of Technology in Boston.

He came to Ohio and began working for B. F. Goodrich in the Aerospace and Defense Products Division in 1928. He and his wife, Dorothy, settled in the Cuyahoga Falls area. As project engineer, he made a high-pressure suit for Wiley Post to use in his high-flying airplane.

However, Colley is most remembered for designing the first U.S. spacesuit. Astronaut Alan B. Shepard, Jr. wore the suit during the first staffed space flight in 1961. In 1994, at the age of 96, Colley received the Distinguished Public Service Medal, the highest civilian award from NASA for his work.

Colley invented the de-icer for aircraft wings, and had 65 patents to his name. He retired from Goodrich in 1962.

Russell was well known for his watercolor paintings and design of silver jewelry. He served as president of the Akron Society of Artists, was a board member of the Cuyahoga Valley Art Center, and was a charter member of Whiskey Painters of America.

Another resident of Cuyahoga Falls was also honored for his work on the space suit. Ray Goodwin, owner of the Goodwin Manufacturing Company, worked closely with B. F. Goodrich on *Project Mercury*. His company worked with the project engineers, such as Colley, to manufacture parts for the suits.

Goodwin, a native of Pennsylvania, moved to Cuyahoga Falls in 1929. He worked for the American Hard Rubber Company in Akron before starting his own business. He had a special interest in the space program because of his background as a test pilot.

Goodwin and Colley were honored, along with other companies that contributed to the achievement of America's first orbital flight, at a special banquet in Columbus, Ohio, in 1962.

* * *

Charles J. Pilliod Jr.
- Business Executive -

Charles J. Pilliod, Jr. was inducted into the Automotive Hall of Fame in recognition of his outstanding contribution to the auto industry. He has been the recipient of numerous international awards. The 1937 Cuyahoga Falls graduate continues to serve on several boards and committees.

Charles J. Pilliod, Jr., retired Chairman of The Goodyear Tire and Rubber Company, has had a long and distinguished career in both industry and government.

Pilliod was born in Cuyahoga Falls in 1918, a few miles from Goodyear's Corporate Headquarters in Akron, Ohio. He joined Goodyear in 1941 as a production trainee. After serving as an Air Force pilot in World War II, he rejoined Goodyear in 1945.

Management positions took him to Goodyear's Latin American operations, and in 1963 he became Managing Director of Goodyear-Great Britain. In 1971 he was elected President of Goodyear International, and he became President and Chief Operating Officer of The Goodyear Tire & Rubber Company in 1972.

Pilliod served as a Director of the U. S. Chamber of Commerce. He served on several national committees and was appointed U.S. Ambassador to Mexico in 1986.

He has been active on the boards of several U.S. companies including: CasTech Aluminum Group, Inc., CPC International, Continental Group, Greyhound Corporation, Diebold, Inc., and others.

In 1946 Pilliod married Betty Jacobs (Falls High class of 1941). They had five children. Betty passed away in 1983. Later Pilliod married Nancy J. Conley who accompanied him when he served in Mexico. Between them, they have eight children.

* * *

Judge Lynn C. Slaby
- Court of Appeals Judge -

Lynn C. Slaby graduated from Cuyahoga Falls High School in 1956. He received a Bachelor of Science Degree in Business Administration, majoring in finance, from the University of Akron in 1967. Continuing his education, he received his Juris Doctorate Degree in 1972 from the University of Akron.

Before becoming an attorney, Judge Slaby was a branch manager for National City Bank and a trust accountant for the Goodyear Bank Trust Department.

Judge Slaby served as Assistant Law Director and Prosecutor for the cities of Akron and Cuyahoga Falls. During his term as Prosecutor in Akron (lasting 14 years) he was active in drafting legislation and testifying before the State and Federal Legislature. He prosecuted several cases that gained national recognition; most notable was Jeffrey Dahmer. Judge Slaby was appointed by Lt. Governor Mike Dewine, Chairman of a statewide committee to study Ohio's not guilty by reason of insanity plea. This has led to a revamping of the system.

Governor George Voinovich appointed Judge Lynn Slaby to the Ninth District Court of Appeals on January 5, 1995. Judge Slaby has participated in over 2,100 cases. He has written over 800 opinions. He has also been assigned by the Chief Justice of the Ohio Supreme Court to hear cases on the Ohio Supreme Court, as well as the Fifth District Court of Appeals.

Judge Slaby has been an active member of many organizations. He is past president of both the National District Attorneys Association and the Ohio Prosecuting Attorneys Association. He serves on the alumni boards of both the College of Law and the Business College at the University of Akron.

Judge Slaby has been an instructor at the University of Akron, The National Judicial College, The National College for Prosecuting Attorneys, the Akron Police Academy, the Summit County Sheriff's Academy, and the American Institute for Paralegal Studies, Inc.

Lynn Slaby, and his wife, Marilyn, have two married daughters and one son.

* * *

Marc Moon AWS
- Artist -

Marc Moon's talent surfaced when he was just a young child in Saskatchewan, Canada. His dad was with General Motors, and the family lived 200 miles north of the Dakotas where the winters were long and boring. A family friend raved over one of young Marc's drawings and paid him a quarter for the artwork. The innate talent blossomed and Marc was destined to become a professional artist.

After graduating from Kenmore High School in Akron, Ohio and serving three years in the Marines, he married Mary Lou Rathbun, his high school sweetheart. They have been together 57 years.

Regardless of how talented a person may be, it is difficult to support a family on talent alone. We have all heard of the "starving artists" and Marc was determined not to be part of that group. He and a partner opened an Art School and were fairly successful for a while. However, there was not enough money generated to support two families, and Marc left the business.

He had purchased a house on 21st Street in 1953 built by the Caporaletti brothers. Now, with a mortgage, a car payment, a wife, three kids and a dog, Marc needed to get serious about the financial situation.

He began teaching watercolor classes at the Cuyahoga Valley Art Center, the Alliance Art Center, and the Canton and Massillon Art Museums. He built a studio in the basement of his house and began giving lessons.

Moon entered a few art shows and began getting recognition. He won twice in Atlantic City. In 1963, Mary Lou and Marc headed to the Virginia Beach Art Show with little more than $40 in their pockets. Not sure if they would be able to pay the motel bill, they were hopeful that they would sell some of Marc's paintings.

It seemed to be the break Moon needed. He won Best of Show and $500. That four-day weekend they sold $3,000 worth of Marc's paintings! He was on his way to being nationally recognized and rewarded for his work.

During his career Marc has conducted watercolor workshops throughout the United States and Canada. For 18 years he traveled to Rockport, Massachusetts, with a group of artists. They painted furiously, often turning out two paintings a day.

He was elected to Signature Membership in the American Watercolor Society in 1963. Other memberships include Ohio Watercolor Society, Georgia Watercolor Society, Akron Society of Artists, Rockport Art Association, and the Watercolor Honor Society.

Moon has received over 95 national and regional awards and is listed in *Who's Who in American Art*. His paintings have been featured in *American Artists Magazine, Forty Watercolorists and How They Work, Ford Times,* and many other national publications.

The Moons' oldest daughter, Lou Ann, inherited her father's talent. She actually took a few lessons from her dad when she was a child. Even then, Marc could tell that she was going to be successful. She has a gallery in Augusta, Georgia, and is the past president of the Georgia Watercolor Society.

Throughout his life and career Marc's philosophy has been, "Success can never be achieved without exposure to failure."

For many years Marc had a studio at 198 Portage Trail. He had an 8,000 square foot gallery, and plenty of room to teach in the building that had previously been a funeral home. Today, Marc and Mary Lou reside in a condo in west Akron where he maintains his studio. Although semi-retired, Marc is painting with his usual enthusiasm and passion.

Marc Moon had a studio at 198 Portage Trail for many years. A founding member of Ohio Watercolor Society, he has conducted workshops throughout the United States and Canada.

* * *

VIII

Education & Inspiration

~ Schools ~

Students Liane Hammack, Mary Ellen Cross, Russell Thomas and Carolyn Crum pledge the flag at Grant Elementary School in the 1940s.

Photo Courtesy of the Cuyahoga Falls Schools Alumni Foundation

147

Education improves the lives of individuals, and societies throughout the ages have looked to scholars to provide leadership. From Plato to Einstein mankind has relied on the knowledge of great minds for direction.

Individuals that have received at least a high school education or are in the skilled trades earn more money during their lifetime than those without education.

The industrialized nations of the world have outdistanced the under-developed and developing countries as a result of education and opportunity. It is through education we discover where we have been, and through education we dare to dream of the future.

Education in the United States comes in a variety of forms and philosophies. We address only the formal education and schooling of the children in the Cuyahoga Falls area. Our thanks to the public and private schools of the city for assisting us with the following information.

Reading, writing and arithmetic were taught on the second floor of a three-story log building in the early 1800s. The building was located on the corner of what is now Broad Boulevard and Front Street. Little is known of this initial arrangement, but it is believed that one large classroom housed children who sat on simple benches made of split logs.

In 1834 J. H. Reynolds opened a private school for boys. Sarah Carpenter opened a school for girls housed in a schoolroom attached to the St. John's Episcopal Church in 1836. In 1837, Rev. Roswell Brooks and Charles Clark established the Cuyahoga Falls Institute at the corner of Portage Trail and Second Street. Now, the Pilgrim Church stands at that location.

In early historical records of Cuyahoga Falls, we find two different time periods when buildings called the **Lyceum** were identified as public places for *literary education.* (Lyceum is a Greek word meaning lecture hall.) It is believed that these buildings were used for town meetings as well as classroom space.

    Cuyahoga Falls constructed several new school buildings during the 1950s and 1960s. Housing allotments were springing up throughout the city bringing in large numbers of young children. As those students completed their education, school buildings closed due to declining enrollment.

Public Schools

Chronology of Cuyahoga Falls City School Buildings

1854 – Cuyahoga Falls School District created.

1870 – **Union School** (later called East School) opened. Purpose was to replace all of the one-room schools in the city. East School was condemned and closed in 1938. Location is now the site of a high rise apartment building.

Broad Street Elementary School, 8 A, 1946
Photo Courtesy of Cuyahoga Falls Historical Society

1908 – **Broad Elementary School** opened, 440 Broad Boulevard. Closed and razed in 1968.

1909 – **Crawford Elementary School** opened, 2379 Third Street. Named for Ellen K. Crawford, an outstanding teacher and school board member who was killed in 1916 as she crossed the interurban tracks on her way to a school board meeting. The building was closed and sold in 1969, and razed in 1972. A high rise apartment building now stands on the Crawford Elementary site.

1919 – **Silver Lake Elementary School** opened, 2970 Overlook Road. Classes were originally held in the Lodge Homestead. The school became part of the Cuyahoga Falls School System in 1965.

1922 – **Cuyahoga Falls High School** opened, 2300 Fourth Street. Opening enrollment 650 students.

A rough and ready Cuyahoga Falls High School football team in the early 1920s.
Photo Courtesy of Taylor Memorial Library

1930 – **Grant Elementary School**, 1201 Grant Street, and **Lincoln Elementary School**, 3131 Bailey Road. The "twin" buildings were constructed from the same set of architect's plans. Grant Elementary was closed in 1983 due to reorganization and the building leased to the city of Cuyahoga Falls. The annual lease is $100, and expires in 2011. The building has been completely renovated and is called the Quirk Cultural Center. Lincoln Elementary is still being used for grades K – 5.

1949 – **Edward Rowland Sill Middle School**, 1910 Searl Street. Opened as an elementary school and was later changed to house junior high age students. Named in honor of Edward R. Sill, famous teacher-poet who also served as Superintendent of Schools and principal of Cuyahoga Falls High School.

1952 – **William H. Richardson Elementary School** opened, 2226 Twenty-third Street. Named to honor William H. Richardson who retired in 1932 having completed forty-seven years in the field of education.

1954 – **Harvey Bolich Middle School** opened, 2630 Thirteenth Street. Named in honor of Harvey O. Bolich who was a teacher and principal.

1956 – **Henry Newberry Elementary School** opened, 2800 Thirteenth Street. Named in honor of the first mayor of the town who later served as a member of the Board of Education.

1959 – **H. A. Preston Elementary School** opened, 800 Tallmadge Road. Named in honor of Henry Alfred Preston, a music teacher at the high school.

1962 – **F. H. Bode Elementary School** opened, 420 Washington Avenue. Named in memory of Cuyahoga Falls City Schools Superintendent, Fred H. Bode. The building was closed in 1983. It was leased to Goodyear

Tire and Rubber Company from 1984-91. The building is now occupied by the Summit County Board of Education, and the Mid Eastern Ohio Special Education Regional Resource Center, MEO-SERRC.

1963 – **Fredrick Schnee Elementary School** opened, 2222 Issaquah Street. Named in honor of Fredrick Schnee who served as Superintendent of Schools for 20 years. The building now houses a Head-Start Program.

1969 – **DeWitt Elementary** opened, 424 Falls Avenue.

The Cuyahoga Falls Black Tigers football team senior squad 2001-2002. The Tigers qualified for the first time in many years to participate in the State Finals.
Photo Courtesy of Cuyahoga Falls High School Athletic Department

1969 – **Gilbert Roberts Middle School** opened, 3333 Charles Street. Named to honor Gilbert Roberts who served the district for 41 years as teacher, coach, principal, and superintendent.

Cuyahoga Falls Schools Alumni Foundation
(Special Thanks to Executive Director Don Miller for assisting with school and alumni information)

A steering committee met in 1983 to discuss forming an organization that would maintain a list of Cuyahoga Falls High School alumni. The group was headed by Superintendent Dr. Harold E. Wilson, and included, Assistant Superintendent William H. Barth, Assistant Superintendent John W. Steinhauer, John David Jones, and Gary Marshall.

The non-profit Cuyahoga Falls Schools Alumni Foundation was incorporated in the spring of 1984. Original Board Members included Judge James Bierce, Douglas Flinn, Gary Marshall, Charles J. Pilliod, Jr., John W. Steinhauer, and Dr. Harold E. Wilson.

By October of that year a computerized mailing list of 18,000 names had been compiled. As of October 2001, the foundation had a list of 29,900 Cuyahoga Falls graduates. The mission of the organization has expanded to include the recognition of distinguished alumni and an Alumni Scholarship Awards Program.

The 2002 Board of Trustees included John L. Jones-President, Christy Mains-Fouser-Vice President, Steven W. Amos and David L. Wilson-Co-Secretaries, William H. Clifford, Sandy E. Krueger, Charles J. Pilliod, Jr., Dr. Bruce Rothmann, Frank Santos, Dave Scarberry, Marj Schlaeppi, Lynn C. Slaby, Ruth E. Smith, John S. Steinhauer, Dr. Richard F. Viering, and Dr. Harold E. Wilson. Don Miller serves as the Executive Director of the Foundation.

* * *

Private Schools

Chapel Hill Christian Schools - Locust Street Christian & Missionary Alliance Church of Akron moved to the Chapel Hill area in the early 1960s. Pastor Robert Turner proposed starting a Christian Day School. A Board of Education was formed; however, there were only 15 prospective students. Therefore the program didn't get off the ground.

Pastor Turner requested help from Christian Schools, Inc. of Seattle, Washington. Under their direction, by April 1966, Mr. and Mrs. Vinton moved to Akron to begin the day to day operations of school preparation. Christian Schools, Inc. was authorized to be the starter and interim operator of Chapel Hill Christian School.

School opened that fall with an enrollment of 109 students in kindergarten through seventh grade. In 1967, Pre-Kindergarten and eight grades were added to the program.

At a special board meeting in 1967, a Christian High School Committee was founded. From this event came the beginning of the Cuyahoga Valley Christian Academy.

Cuyahoga Valley Christian Academy (CVCA) was opened as a Junior/Senior High School. The grade school enrollment at Chapel Hill Christian School (CHCS) was 315 for the 1969-70 school year. Enrollment continued to increase and eventually it was decided to open another campus. Property was acquired south of Akron.

During the 2001-02 school year, approximately 371 students were enrolled at the North campus on Howe Road, and 204 students were enrolled at the South campus on East Turkeyfoot Road in the City of Green.

Cuyahoga Valley Christian Academy – Cuyahoga Valley Christian Academy (CVCA) started as an outgrowth of Chapel Hill Christian School (CHCS). Ten men, who had been associated with Chapel Hill Christian School, and who were committed to exploring possibilities for a Christian secondary school, met regularly for 1½ years.

CVCA was incorporated in 1968, but it was necessary to secure funding and locate a site. Consideration was given to 6½ acres of land in Tamsin Park. However, a more desirable plot, 30 acres, was found on Wyoga Lake Road and the project was underway.

Fundraising produced just over $500,000 in pledges and bonds, and ground was broken and construction started in March 1969. The building was not completed in time for school to start that fall, so the School Board had to look for an alternative location for the 198 students.

Crawford Elementary School, an abandoned and condemned grade school building was rented from the city. Stories are told of that winter at Crawford when the old, worn out coal furnace blew soot throughout the building. Board members would arrive at the school between 5:00 and 6:00 a.m. to *tend to the furnace and pray.*

In May 1970, classes were moved to the new facility. A science wing was added, along with additional classrooms and a gymnasium as enrollment increased.

CVCA had continued to grow. Enrollment 2001-2002 for grades seven through twelve was 800 students. Jon F. Holley served as Head Master with Roger Taylor as Administrator.

Walsh Jesuit High School – Jane Jordon Walsh, the widow of Cornelius M. Walsh, a prominent industrialist and resident of Cuyahoga Falls, left the bulk of her estate to the Jesuits for the creation of a high school. The two million dollars remained in a trust until 1958, when nephew, William Walsh, became involved in seeing that the money was put into the hands of those who could help.

The Diocese of Cleveland added one million dollars to the Walsh fund, and the greater Akron area was soon to have a Catholic, college preparatory high school. One hundred acres of farmland was purchased from Louise and Joseph Conway, and the first all male student body entered the new building on Wyoga Lake Road in 1965.

It took until 1993 for Walsh Jesuit High School to become a co-educational facility, encouraging the enrollment of female students. Today, the student body consists of 50% girls. The school is open to all races and faiths who meet its academic and character requirements.

A worldwide network of Jesuit high schools, colleges and universities serves more than 1.5 million students.

The enrollment for the 2001-2002 school year at Walsh Jesuit High School in Cuyahoga Falls was 860. The student body represented 100 different grade schools within a seven county area. Tuition was $6,225, plus general fees of $200.

~ ~ ~

~Places of Worship~

Whether it is called a house of worship, house of prayer, cathedral, temple, church, synagogue, mosque or a tabernacle, it is the place where man worships his God.

Throughout history, religion has played an important part in the personal lives of all social beings. Groups of various sizes gather to sing praises, read the word, listen to religious leaders, and offer prayers to the Almighty.

When settlers moved to the Western Reserve from the east, they brought with them strong beliefs and a faith that helped to sustain them in this rugged territory. Packed in the boxes and barrels of personal belongings were their prayer books, Bibles and other religious items that helped to uphold their faith.

Religious meetings were often all day events held in private homes. Not only was the gathering a time of worship, but it often served as a social function. Lunch was prepared and served by the ladies, men had an opportunity to share the latest news, and the children and young folks enjoyed each other's company. This *Day of Rest* was important in the life of the early settler.

Eventually, churches of log construction began to appear on the horizon. Often towns built multi-purpose structures that could be used by all denominations.

While local lay leaders usually served the congregation, occasionally a traveling preacher would stop by to perform weddings and baptisms. If lucky, a town might expect the circuit preacher every six to eight weeks. Of course, when he arrived, it was a grand ol' meeting.

An article from the *Times Press 1938* tells of the struggles of the small Magnolia Methodist congregation. The staunch Methodists continued meeting for seventeen years. "Only during the summer when mosquitoes, breeding in the lowland around the building, swarmed around the church, have services been discontinued."

The Cuyahoga Falls community was fortunate to be given a parcel of land for the sole purpose of building churches in the center of town. In 1834, Judge Joshua Stow offered financial support, and a block of land between what is now Portage Trail and Stow Street, and Second and Third Streets, making it possible for three churches to be built in the center of the bustling little town of Cuyahoga Falls.

The designated plot in the middle of the town square soon acquired the title *church square.* The name for that parcel of land continues to be used in the twenty-first century.

Early churches erected in *church square* were the First Christian Church of Cuyahoga Falls, The First United Methodist Church of Cuyahoga Falls (also known as First Church) and St. John's Episcopal Church.

In looking at ways congregations support the ongoing work of the church, we find the following examples of stewardship used in some of the Cuyahoga Falls churches. In the mid-1800s *slip rentals* were a means of bringing money into the church. It was the practice of collecting money from the members based on the pews or *slips* in which they preferred to sit. (The more costly pews were located near the front of the church.)

Weekly offerings, dinners, bazaars, strawberry festivals, and the selling of everything from cheese to the *Guinness Book of World Records* has been tried over the years. During especially difficult financial times, committees would canvass members using signed and sealed pledge cards. If the pledges were not fulfilled, occasionally legal steps were taken.

The number one priority of a church is to meet the spiritual needs of its congregation. A variety of programs to support the body of believers comes by way of weekly worship services, musical ministries, Christian Education, Sunday Schools, Bible studies, youth group activities, television ministries, missions, and other inspirational activities.

All denominations have activities to enrich the lives of those who attend their church, and most churches have programs that reach out into the neighboring community.

Residents of Cuyahoga Falls are fortunate to have many social service programs provided by churches that include; pre-school, before and after school care, day care for adult senior citizens, free meals for those in need, food banks, clothing closets, Red Cross Bloodmobile, space for Summit County Board of Elections, and other activities that benefit local citizens.

Short histories of the churches of Cuyahoga Falls who responded to our inquiry are included; however, limited space restricts the listing of all the spiritual and social programs offered by each congregation.

Bailey Road Christian Church
3200 Bailey Road
Pastor – Rev. Charles F. Mills
Membership – 100

Church services and a picnic were held in 1954 at the Octagonal Shelter House in Virginia Kendall Park. The possibility of establishing a church on the east side of Cuyahoga Falls was discussed.

A second meeting was held at the Y.W.C.A., and Rev. Byron Bankes became the pastor of the small congregation. For the next seven years worship services were held at Lincoln Elementary School.

Building property was purchased in 1955 at the corner of Bailey Road and Madison Avenue, but the first service was not held in the new church until 1961. Construction costs were $90,000, plus another $10,300 was spent for the purchase of 1.3 acres of land.

The Community Church of Christ changed its name to Bailey Road Christian Church. Rev. John Dalton became the first full time pastor in 1958. By the 15th anniversary of the church the membership numbered 245. Rev. Ralph S. Wearstler served the congregation from 1982-1994.

Bethany United Church of Christ
1235 Broad Boulevard
Pastor – Rev. Steve Gehlert
Membership – 650

Bethany United Church of Christ was founded in Akron in 1917 under the name of Avon Street Reformed Church. Seven years later the name was changed from Avon Street to Bethany. In 1927, under the leadership of Rev. J. Theodore Bucher, Bethany Reformed Church moved to Cuyahoga Falls.

Because of nationwide denominational changes, the Cuyahoga Falls church has had several name changes. In 1934 it became Bethany Evangelical and Reformed Church. When the Evangelical and Reformed Church consolidated with the Congregational Christian Churches in 1957, the name Bethany United Church of Christ was adopted.

A local landmark, Bethany's buildings include a beautiful Gothic sanctuary, classrooms, offices, gymnasium, and lounge. It was determined that additional space was badly needed in the early 1990s. The congregation approved construction costs of $1,467,460, and the contract was awarded to Seese/Sveda Construction Company in 1995. The project included remodeling, additional classrooms, a music room, and a new social hall.

Broadman Baptist Church
350 East Bath Road

On April 25, 1951, eight people joined under the leadership of the Rev. Hoyt Douglas for the first service of what would become Broadman Baptist Church. They met in Crawford Elementary School as an Independent Baptist Church. Later they moved to Sackett Street into a building lovingly referred to as *The Warehouse.*

In 1955 they joined the Southern Baptist Convention. A year later, the Falls Baptist Chapel, as it was then called, adopted its present name, Broadman Baptist Church, to be more easily recognized as a Southern Baptist congregation.

The group moved to Newberry Elementary School on 13th Street, and in 1958 purchased a church site on East Bath Road. The cost of the initial construction of the new building was $67,000. In 1964 an education wing was dedicated.

Several different ministers served the congregation over the years. In 1990, the Rev. Jeffery Warren Scott, an Akron native, became pastor. The church began focusing on areas of social concern through a child advocacy ministry and a Hmong fellowship.

Chapel Hill Church
1160 Howe Avenue
Pastor – Rev. Jeff Miller
Membership – 200

The Chapel Hill Church is part of a larger denomination known as the Christian and Missionary Alliance. Around 1890, Mrs. Grace Butts, while living in New York City, sent her parents in Akron literature explaining the doctrine and work of the Alliance. They began holding prayer meetings in the city and surrounding towns.

The first church building was constructed in 1914 on Locust Street. The Rev. S. M. Gerow was the pastor, and the church sent out its first missionary, Miss Edna Hanna, to Argentina in the fall of 1916.

In 1960 the congregation purchased six acres of property, that had been the former site of an 1845 Welsh Church, at the corner of Howe and Brittain Roads. Several additions were made to the original building as the church grew. Under the leadership of Rev. Robert P.

Turner and Rev. Paul Bersche, Chapel Hill Christian School was opened in 1966.

Church In The Falls
837 Chestnut Boulevard
Pastors – Rev. Mark Brazle and Rev. Rod Sheldon
Membership - 300

A worship service was held in a home on Reed Avenue in 1943. The group purchased a building on 4th Street that had been gutted by fire, and set to work donating time, energy and money to restore the building. A full-time minister, Robert Myers, was hired. Church deacons included Lowell Cameron, Frank Feldman and Don Fisk.

L.J. Nicklas was the preacher for most of the 1950s. The church was known as a *Singing Church*, hosting many of the area wide *singings*. However, the congregation was outgrowing the 4th Street building, and it was time to consider a new church building. Property was purchased on Chestnut Boulevard in 1966, exactly 23 years to the day when original members met in the house on Reed Avenue in 1943.

Before long, the new building was underway. On August 6, 1967, the doors to the building were opened for the first Vacation Bible School, and over 400 children attended.

The church has always been mission-minded and helped spread God's word throughout the world. In the 1970s they helped to establish churches in Minerva, Ohio; Glen Falls, New York; and Wooster Avenue in Akron, Ohio. They also helped a young couple named Brazle who went to Belgium to begin mission work.

Community of Believers Church
2543 State Road
Pastor – Tom Bloom
Membership – 450

The Community of Believers Church began as a ministry outreach on the campus of Kent State University. Ted Evans, a director of the Apostolic Team Ministries, founded the church in 1978. Services were held in rented facilities until 1995, when the group purchased the former State Road Theatre.

Open house was held at the newly renovated facility in 1997. The congregation has grown from a handful of committed Christians to a multifaceted community of believers. This non-denominational, Bible-believing church identifies itself as *charismatic-evangelical*.

The Community of Believers Church finally found a permanent home when they purchased the former State Road Theatre in 1995. The theatre had been owned by the Sony Corporation and seated 1,800 people. The movie theatre, popular from the 1950-80s, was remolded by the apostolic ministry that had its beginning in the 1970s at Kent State University.

Postcard Photo Courtesy of Pete Mellinger

Cuyahoga Falls Church of the Nazarene
330 East Bath Road
Pastor – Dave Johnston
Membership – 275

In 1949 the District Nazarene Young People's Society purchased property on the corner of 2nd and Wadsworth Streets. A metal 28-foot by 60-foot building was constructed, and a revival under the direction of the Rev. N. M. Israelson of Kansas City, Missouri, was held at the Nazarene Chapel in 1950.

In 1965 the group moved to its present location on East Bath Road, and built a new facility for the cost of $68,000. Again in 1979, under the leadership of Rev. Ken Culbertson, construction was under way for a fellowship hall and major remodeling of the sanctuary.

As the church leaders considered the increasing demand for additional space in 1987, it was decided that more property was needed. One acre of land adjacent to the church was purchased.

An 8,960 square foot facility was added in 1989. The additional classrooms, kitchen, restrooms, Sunday School office, and new entrance were completed for approximately $350,000. The Rev. David Johnston began serving the congregation in 1983.

First Christian Church Of Cuyahoga Falls
2253 3rd. Street
Membership – 450

One of the oldest churches, the First Christian Church of Cuyahoga Falls, located on *church square*, had its beginning over 120 years ago due to the conviction of two men. Anson Wheeler, of Cuyahoga Falls, and William Southmayd, of Stow, attended the Stow Christian Church.

They thought that a church should be established in Cuyahoga Falls and began holding meetings in homes. Before long, the young church needed more space, and for over six years the men rented various rooms in the center of Cuyahoga Falls.

In 1880 Leonard Southmayd was hired as a half time preacher. Membership was 75, with 44 of those transferred from the Stow Church. The church received its charter in 1884, and the first building, a 30-foot by 40-foot structure, was dedicated in 1885.

Over the years numerous pastors have served the congregation at the First Christian Church. Some stayed only a few months, while others held the position for several years. C.J. Tannar, Professor Bailey Dean of Hiram College, D. W. Besaw, W. L. Denslow, H. H. Tilock, and his son Fred Tilock, Howard Short, Ira Paternoster, and Charles L. Wells are a few of the memorable names.

None of the ministers, however, can match the record of the church organist, Phyllis Leiner, who has been playing music for the congregation for 41 years.

Many additions were made to the original building. Finally, in 1929, ground was broken for a new church. Unfortunately, the Stock Market crashed in October of that year, and by the time the building was completed the entire country was in the midst of the *Great Depression.*

The bankrupt church became a mission church of the Ohio Society, and received help from that organization, as well as the Summit County Disciples Union.

Having survived the trauma of bankruptcy, the church progressed spiritually, and membership increased. Ground was broken in 1962 for much needed educational space, and again in 1980 an additional educational wing was added.

First Christian Church of Cuyahoga Falls was founded over 120 years ago. Located on *church square*, the congregation survived the lean years when the Stock Market crashed and the church struggled with financing the new building.

First Church of Christ, Scientist
2390 4th Street

The First Church of Christ, Scientist is a branch of The First Church of Christ, Scientist of Boston, Massachusetts, founded in 1879. The Cuyahoga Falls church had its beginning in 1929. Local trustees were Grace A. Shephard, E.R. Jones, Bertha M. Fox, B.D. Etz, and Maude V. Botzum.

Its purpose is to promote the teaching and practice of the religion of Christian Science as taught and practiced by its founder, Mary Baker Eddy. The membership elects lay Readers to conduct Sunday and Wednesday services.

First United Methodist Church of Cuyahoga Falls (FIRST CHURCH)

245 Portage Trail
Pastor Rev. Marvin R. Brown
Membership – 4000

First Church, a United Methodist Congregation, was founded in 1830. Services were held in a school building on the corner of Front Street and Wadsworth Avenue. Rev. John McLain, a circuit rider from the Twinsburg circuit, organized the small group, or class, of Methodists. In 1840 the Cuyahoga Falls Methodist Episcopal Church was given "station" status, a step up from the circuit classification.

The first permanent building for the First Church congregation was erected in 1840 on its present site, on a parcel of land donated by Judge Joshua Stow.

In 1920 the original building was replaced by a larger structure, and in 1952, an education building was added. The present sanctuary was added in 1965.

The 172-year history of First Church indicates that more than 60 ministers followed the circuit preacher, McClain. Most of the early pastors served only a year or two. The Rev. Forrest J. Waller D.D. stayed longer than most, and led the congregation from 1982-2001.

First Church is the largest United Methodist congregation in the East Ohio Conference. With a membership of 4,000, it now has a senior pastor, as well as a paid staff of 24 who help to serve the congregation and operate a pre-school for approximately 100 children.

Grace Summit Community

2960 Bailey Road
Pastor – Mike Marette
Membership – 120

The contemporary group of worshipers on Bailey Road has experienced several relocations since the founding of their church in 1989. They began meeting at the Quirk Center and moved in 1992 to a daycare center in Stow. In 1995 the roof of the daycare building collapsed, and it was necessary to look for a new place to worship.

Grace Covenant Community Church had purchased a building at 2960 Bailey Road. That group agreed to allow the misplaced congregation to use the Bailey Road building when it was not in use. In 1996 the two congregations merged.

Graham Road Baptist Church
705 Graham Road
Pastor – Larry D. Engle
Membership – 360

In the spring of 1923, a group of neighbors met in a home located in the 700 block of Graham Road to discuss the formation of a church in the Stow-Cuyahoga Falls community. The Rev. A.M. Dixon led the group, and soon the small body of believers found a building that was once a chicken coop where they could meet.

By 1926 the church was recognized as a duly constituted New Testament Baptist Church with a charter membership of 25. The church is in fellowship with the General Association of Regular Baptist Churches that is made up of over 1,400 Independent Baptist churches.

Graham Road Baptist Church attendance began to increase, and the present building was constructed in 1962 under the leadership of Pastor Ben C. Jennings. In 1980 the church, with a membership of 360, invited Pastor Larry D. Engle to become the head pastor.

Graham Road Baptist had its beginning in a former chicken coop in 1923. Sunday morning worshipers are shown here with the Rev. Larry Engle (far right) who has been the pastor at Graham Road Baptist Church since 1980.

Grandview United Methodist Church
2315 Phelps Avenue
Pastor – Rev. Bruce Morrison
Membership – 250

In 1946 the Evangelical Church and the United Brethren in Christ Church merged. The merger put two Evangelical United Brethren Churches within two blocks of each other.

The church congregation, located at the corner of Tallmadge Avenue and Dayton Street, voted to come to Cuyahoga Falls and build a new church on property that had been owned by the denomination for a number of years.

Thus in 1948, in the midst of the post-war building boom (when the Buena Vista Allotment was being built)

39 adults and children joined the Cuyahoga Falls group. The first service was held in a large rented tent with the Rev. Faye G. Reese leading the congregation.

That first winter, the small but loyal fellowship moved into a surplus army barracks located where the present church parking lot is today. Ground breaking was held in 1948 for a new building on Phelps Avenue. The congregation began to grow, and the Rev. James B. Wolf, fresh out of seminary, served the group from 1953-91. Rev. Milton Smith was pastor from 1991-94.

In 1966 the present sanctuary, fellowship hall and remodeling of the entire facility was undertaken for a cost of $170,000. Another merger faced the congregation when the Evangelical United Brethren Church and the Methodist Church joined in 1968 to form the United Methodist Church. Rev. Bruce Morrison was called to serve the congregation in 1994.

Immaculate Heart of Mary Catholic Church
1905 Portage Trail
Pastor – Father Thomas W. McCann
Membership – 2,000 families
School - 540

Immaculate Heart of Mary Parish was established in 1952 with Father Thomas D. McIntyre as the appointed pastor. The State Theater on State Road was the meeting place for the 471 families of the parish. A four-hour whirlwind fund drive raised pledges of $110,000 for the building of a church and school.

The church and school were built consecutively for a cost of $456,000, and the first Mass was celebrated in the new building on Portage Trail in 1954. A rectory was completed in 1955 and a convent was added in 1958. By 1959 the school accommodated 850 students.

In 1987 the convent was leased to Elder Day Care and Respite Center, as a hospice for elderly needing daytime care or assisted living.

Bishop Pilla presided over the consecration of the church in 1993. Recent additions and improvements to IMH included new stained glass windows, Stations of the Cross, as well as the Parish Community Center.

Father John Rathfon replaced Father McIntyre in 1978. Father Thomas W. McCann became the third pastor of the large parish in 1994. Kim Green is principal of the school with an enrollment of over 500 students and 18 full-time school teachers.

Islamic Society of Akron and Kent
152 East Steels Corners Road
Chairman - Dr. Ihsan Ul Haque, MD
Acting Principal of grades K-4 – Yasar Dhahar

This Islamic Society had its modest beginnings when a group of Muslim students at Kent State University established a small masjid or mosque in their apartment in 1979. Muslims from adjoining communities joined them, and a Sunday Islamic School was started with an enrollment of eight children.

The group rented a house on Williams Street and moved the masjid there in 1980. The Islamic Society of Greater Kent was formally established in 1981. After another move, the Society was able to purchase an old church building on Crain Avenue in Kent in 1985. Extensive work was done to the building to convert it to a masjid, and an open house was held for Muslims and Non-Muslims.

Space was limited, and the Society began looking for a plot of land that would suit their needs. They found the perfect location at 152 East Steels Corners Road, and began the construction of the new Islamic Center Project in September 1996.

The new Center cost approximately $2.5 million and consists of three parts; the Masjid, the Islamic School, and the Multi-purpose Hall.

Muslim students of the University of Akron had established a masjid in a rented house on Powers Street in Akron in 1985. Other Muslims from the surrounding communities joined them, and in 1995 the Islamic Society of Akron (ISA) and the Islamic Society of Greater Kent (ISGK) merged to form the Islamic Society of Akron and Kent (ISAK).

Muslims from the Islamic Society of Akron (ISA) and the Islamic Society of Greater Kent (ISGK) merged in 1995 to form the Islamic Society of Akron and Kent (ISAK). The center on East Steels Corners Road consists of the Masjid, the Islamic School and the Multi-purpose Hall.

North Haven Evangelical Covenant Church
2679 North Haven Boulevard
Pastor – Rev. Corey Johnsrud

In 1952, Miss Pansy Ostberg, a Middle East Conference parish worker, helped to organize those interested in forming a new Covenant Church. The group of 14 held its first Sunday School meeting in the basement of Harold Carlson's home. Rev. Donald Pearson began serving the congregation of 16 in 1953.

Charter members included Mr. & Mrs. Adolph Anderson, Mr. & Mrs. Harold Carlson, Mr. & Mrs. Donald Griffith, Mr. & Mrs. Robert Hahn, Mr. & Mrs. C. Raymond Johnson, Douglas Johnson, Mr. & Mrs. Gust Kallstrom, Mr. & Mrs. John Laing, Mr. & Mrs. James McIntyre, Rev. & Mrs. Donald Pearson, and Mr. & Mrs. Gunnar Wahlgren.

A parsonage-chapel structure was built that took advantage of the double garage-breezeway, basement and bedroom space, using them for meeting rooms. Because of overcrowding, classes were being held in neighboring homes by early in 1954.

The congregation was anxious for a larger facility, and ground breaking for a new building was held in the fall of 1957. By 1960 the church became self-supporting and no longer needed the financial support of the Middle East Conference. By the 10th anniversary in 1963 the membership had grown to 135.

Northampton Baptist Church
333 West Steels Corners Road
Pastor – Franklin A. Lorenz
Membership – 300

A handful of believers met in the Northampton Town Hall under the leadership of Pastor Franklin Lorenz in 1956. By the fall of 1959 the growing congregation was ready to break ground for a new church building on West Steels Corners Road. Easter Sunday, 1960, was a time of celebration as the worshippers held the first service in their own building.

The need to expand led to the enlargement of the auditorium and additional Sunday School rooms in 1965. The growing congregation built a new sanctuary in 1973, and added another wing to the building in 1997. Pastor Lorenz continues to lead the church with the help of additional ministers.

Northampton United Methodist Church
825 West Bath Road
Pastor – Rev. Dave Scavuzzo
Membership – 520
Pre-school enrollment - 70

The Northampton United Methodist Church grew out of camp meetings held in farm homes throughout the community. The Sunday School was flourishing as far back as 1831, even though there were only 30 log houses between Akron and Northampton.

In 1855, the Methodists and members of the township began construction of a church building on one-half acre of land donated by Reese Jones. Trustees included: O. F. Rice, Isaac Scott, S. W. Harrington, S. R. Perkins, Elisha Prior, and Samuel McLoney.

The church boasted a 75-foot tall steeple, high pulpit and pews. The congregation merged in 1856 with the Congregationalists, and became a Union Church.

In 1880 services were discontinued. Later the Rev. R. Smith began preaching and refurbishing the building. Records indicate a homecoming was held in 1920. An educational wing was built in 1964, and the sanctuary and the educational wing were enlarged in 1982.

A tornado severely damaged the old portion of the building in 1992. It was necessary for the congregation to meet elsewhere, and Woodridge Middle School served as a home for the group until repairs were made.

Until now, the largest period of growth was in the 1970s and early 1980s under the ministry of Dr. Yoost. From 1984-90 attendance and membership were down. Since 1990 the congregation has experienced rapid and steady growth.

There were only 30 log houses between Akron and the rural Northampton community when the Northampton United Methodist Church had its beginning in 1831.

Northminster Presbyterian Church
104 W. Portage Trail Ext.
Pastor – Rev. David L. Herron
Membership – 285

In 1953, Richardson School was the meeting place for a Presbyterian mission church led by the Rev. Richard R. Eshler of Pennsylvania. The organized group anticipated the uniting of the Presbyterian Church in the U.S.A. and the United Presbyterian Church.

A successful building campaign was held in 1954, and ground was broken for the new church on West Portage Trail Extension in 1956. The first worship service was held in the new sanctuary on Palm Sunday, March 31, 1957. An education wing was dedicated in 1962, and in 1990 a fellowship hall was built.

Rev. Charles W. Evans began serving Northminister in 1968, and Dr. Joseph W. Atkins served from 1972 through 1998. Pastor Dave Herron replaced interim pastors in January 2001.

Eight of the 142 original charter members are still living in the Cuyahoga Falls area: Mr. & Mrs. Charles S. Hamlet, Mr. & Mrs. Paul Lyons, Mr. & Mrs. John Bowen, Babette Wasnac Robinson, and Janet Tussing.

Pilgrim United Church of Christ
130 Broad Blvd.
Pastor – Rev. Kirk W. Bruce
Membership – 370

In 1833, a meeting was held at the log schoolhouse on Broad and 2nd Streets to discuss the formation of the Congregationalist Church. Community leaders Elisha Sill, Henry Newberry, Birdsey Booth, Jabez Hamlin, Ogden Wetmore, Fredrick Upson, the Rev. Benson C. Baldwin, and "several ladies" were in attendance.

The First Congregational Church of Cuyahoga Falls was founded in 1834. Beginning in 1835 the group met for 12 years in the community owned building called the *Lyceum*.

In 1847 a new church building was erected on Broad Boulevard. The foundation stones were quarried from sandstone from the Cuyahoga Falls gorge. It is one of the oldest buildings in Summit County and was entered on the National Register of Historical Places by the

United States Department of Interior and the National Park Services in 1976.

Pilgrim United Church of Christ was built over 150 years ago with materials quarried from the Gorge. It is one of the oldest churches in continuous use in Summit County.
Photo Courtesy of Marj Schlaeppi

The building is of neo-classical design, and is adorned with a tall spire, typical of New England Congregational Churches. Additions enlarged the complex over the years. Electric lights were installed in 1892 with notices posted to remind everyone that it was not necessary to light the fixtures, and, that the illumination presented no danger to health.

Rev. Benson C. Baldwin, a circuit preacher commissioned by the Home Missionary Society in Boston, served as the first pastor of the church. Every other week he preached at an Akron church. From 1836-1838 Rev. Joel Byington served the congregation for an annual salary of $700. A merger in 1965 resulted in the name change to Pilgrim United Church of Christ.

Redeemer Lutheran Church
2141 Fifth Street
Pastor – Rev. Keith Johnson & Rev. Larry Leuthaeuser
Membership – 1,150
School Enrollment - 250

Redeemer Lutheran Church had its first meetings, as did many early churches, in private homes. First organized in 1916, the small group was led by a native Akronite, William Single, a graduate of Concordia Seminary. Assigned as a missionary to start a new church in the Falls, Single met with 27 persons at the home of Mrs. Pauline Schlichter on Brick Street. Mr. and Mrs. Christ Feucht, Sr. offered their home as a meeting place for services to be held twice monthly.

By May 1917, the congregation needed a larger meeting place. Over the next couple of years the group met at the Weller Funeral Home, and the Chamber of Commerce Hall on Front Street.

In 1918 the first formal church organization was created, and for $5,000, the group purchased a site for a permanent church. In 1920 the congregation moved to the stone church on Fourth Street.

Reverend Single moved to Dover, Ohio, in 1922, and the Reverend Theodore E. Prinz ministered to the congregation for many rewarding years. Records indicate that when Pastor Prinz came to the Falls pastorate, the congregation numbered about 15 families. By 1947 the congregation numbered close to 500.

In April 1949 the interior of the church was completely destroyed by fire. It was necessary to find another place to worship, and the Falls Theater and St. Paul's Episcopal Church offered space.

The new church on Fifth Street was dedicated in 1950. The K-8 grade school was opened in 1958. In 1965 the present church was constructed, and in 1994 an additional building was added to the school facility.

St. Eugene's Catholic Church
1821 Munroe Falls Avenue
Pastor – Rev. Neil A. Crosby
Membership – 900 families

In 1963 the parish was formed and the first Masses were held at the former Schnee School building on Issaquah Avenue. The Reverend William A. Winchester was appointed pastor of the new congregation.

Property was acquired on Munroe Falls Avenue, and construction was soon underway. The new church was ready for occupancy in 1964. The Reverend John J. Kilcoyne was appointed to serve the parish in 1973, and stayed in that position until 1978 when Reverend B. Thomas Zeisig took over.

In 1981, St Eugene's Social Hall was built to accommodate the growing congregation. The church celebrated its 25th anniversary in 1988. A wide group of parishioners of diverse ages and interests come to St. Eugene's Catholic Church from Stow, Munroe Falls and the Cuyahoga Falls area.

St. John's Episcopal Church

2220 Second Street
Pastor – Rev. Donna Hayhow
Membership – 400

Josiah Wetmore, his devout Episcopalian wife Nancy, and their children came to the Western Reserve in 1818. When neighbors gathered on Sundays, Nancy read from the prayer book and Josiah read from a book of sermons. A missionary priest, the Rev. Roger Searle, visited often to administer Holy Communion and to baptize individuals.

The Reverends James McElroy and E.E. Lyster organized St. John's Episcopal Church in 1830. The name for the church was chosen by Mrs. Asa Stanley, who had come to the area from a church of the same name in Canandaigua, New York. The location of the first building was in Stow, near what is now Wetmore Park. It was a log cabin shared with several other denominations.

Judge Joshua Stow donated a block of land between Portage Trail and Stow Street, and Second and Third Streets to encourage the building of churches in the local public square. He offered the Episcopalian and the Methodist congregations $250 each, and a prime location for the construction of the stately church buildings.

The white frame St John's Episcopal Church was erected in 1835. It measured 66 feet by 42 feet and cost $3,200 to build. In 1907 the building was razed to make way for the current church building of English Gothic design.

The congregation moved into the new building in 1909. The bell in the tower was purchased in 1884 and is still used today. The wooden cross, hanging above the bell tower pews, was made by William Tompkin in 1974 from a tree from the John and Michael Nabors farm on Hardy Road.

The spectacular stained glass memorial windows of the church create an atmosphere of awe for worshipers. The Christ the Shepherd window, was the first memorial window dedicated in 1887. Additional windows have been given in the name of loved ones over the years.

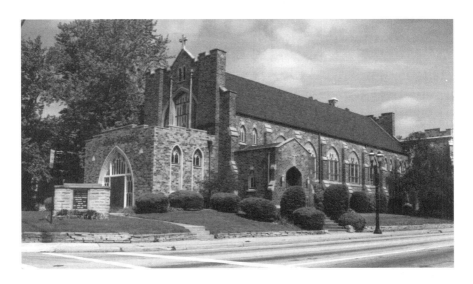

Stained glass memorial windows and English Gothic architecture make the century old St. John's Episcopal Church one of the most attractive buildings in the city.

St. Joseph Church Of Cuyahoga Falls
1761 Second Street
Pastor – Father James J. Marsick
Membership – 2,000 families
School – Grades K-8, 400 students

Dominican priests visited a handful of Catholic families in their Cuyahoga Falls homes in 1831. By 1836 the village had a population of 1,200, and the Catholic Church in this area was considered a station church. In 1867 the church became a mission of the Hudson parish of St. Mary's.

In 1893 Father Patrick Barry, the resident pastor, purchased land at the corner of 2nd and Sackett Streets for the building of a church. The 30-foot by 60-foot building was completed at a cost of $2,000. The little mission church was comprised of twenty Catholic families.

It is interesting to note that in 1907 the yearly income of the parish was about $550. But the church was rapidly outgrowing its available space. Parishioners pledged $3,120 in 1911 for a new and larger building. Dedication was held in September 1913 for the new church that could seat 340 people.

In 1922 Cornelius M. Walsh donated $15,000, and purchased property at the corner of Third Street and Falls Avenue for a parish school. The Sisters of Charity of St. Augustine arrived in the fall of 1923, and the school enrollment climbed to 185 pupils. With students coming from Tallmadge and Stow, school enrollment reached its peak in 1960, with 1,270 students attending St. Joseph's.

Over the years several major building projects have enlarged the school and church. St. Joseph's members actively supported the ongoing work of the parish. Many men who were out of work donated their labor, during the difficult time of the "Great Depression", to the church expansion project.

In 1933, the church added additional seating as well as a bell tower with a 1,000-pound McNeely bell and a Seth Thomas eight-day clock.

In 1978, because of the deteriorating physical condition of the church building, a Church Renovation Program was initiated. St. Joseph's Church celebrated its 150th anniversary in 1983, and again upgraded facilities.

St. Luke's Lutheran (E.L.C.A.) Church
2121 6ᵗʰ Street
Pastor – Rev. Robert E. Linsz
Membership – 420

St. Luke's Evangelical Lutheran Church had its beginning in 1946 when Pastor Nevin B. Stover was appointed by the Board of American Missions as mission developer. Cuyahoga Falls High School auditorium served as the location for the first worship service with approximately 100 individuals in attendance.

In 1947 the church received its charter, and Nevin B. Stover began his 30-year pastorship at St. Luke's. In 1948 property was purchased on Sixth Street, and two years later ground was broken for the building of the present church. An educational unit was added in 1956 and the sanctuary dedicated in 1962.

John Herrlinger served as senior pastor from 1977 to 1998. Robert E. Linsz became the senior pastor at St. Luke's in 1999.

Trinity United Methodist Church
755 Howe Avenue
Pastor – Rev. Brian A. Morrison
Membership – 130

Around 1925 a group of Cuyahoga Falls Christians began worshiping together under the direction of lay leaders. They called themselves the Magnolia Church, and met in a building at the corner of Orchard and Avery Streets. In the 1930s, George Mayer, who was addressed as reverend, served as pastor of the small group.

Superintendent Stanley Mullins of the Northeast Methodist Conference met with the congregation and talked with them about joining the Methodist group. Finally, in 1958 the Magnolia group made the decision to affiliate themselves with the Methodists, and renamed their church Trinity Methodist. Later the name was changed to Trinity United Methodist Church.

The congregation moved their meeting place to Sill School and later to Preston Elementary School. In 1965 under the leadership of Rev. Robert Raynes, the church purchased five acres of property from the city. Long time members recall that part of the land had at one time been used as a city dump, or landfill. But the property was available, and the church had found a place of its own.

United Presbyterian Church
2819 Hudson Drive
Membership – 460

Prior to 1914 there were not any churches in the developing north end of Cuyahoga Falls. Before moving to the area, Mrs. Irena McKenzie and family had attended the United Presbyterian Church at Metz (a former community in the vicinity of Hudson Drive and McCauley Road). Mrs. Cora Bolender and family had moved from Ellet, where they had attended a United Presbyterian Church.

Their children walked Sunday morning and evening to the Methodist Church downtown, since that was the nearest place of worship. The two neighbors felt there was a need for a church in their own area.

With the assistance of the North Hill United Presbyterian Church and the Metz church, the North End United Presbyterian Sabbath School held its first session in the Crawford Elementary School. Soon the basement of the new church on Hudson Drive was finished, and services were held there. By 1916 the congregation was organized with 48 charter members led by the Rev. J. S. Dague.

Dr. Henry Orr Lietman served the congregation from 1948 until his death in 1964. During this time housing developments were bringing many new families to the community. In 1949 ground was broken for the current church. In 1957 a new sanctuary was added.

A church was needed on the north end of town in the early 1900s, and two women are credited with leading the campaign to organize a local Presbyterian Church on Hudson Drive.

Word of His Grace Fellowship
110 East Steels Corners Road
Pastor – John Rasicci
Membership – 200

Pastor John Rasicci graduated from Rhema Bible Training Center in 1980 and was ordained through Grace Fellowship in Tulsa, Oklahoma. He felt called to start a church.

The Word of Grace Fellowship was started in 1983 with a grand total of nine people meeting in the living room of a private home in Cuyahoga Falls. The small group worked to increase membership and soon moved to the Knights of Columbus Hall. Eventually they moved to larger quarters at Preston Elementary School.

The congregation purchased five acres of land on Steels Corners Road and held their first service in the newly constructed church building in 1991. In 1994, another door of opportunity opened for them to purchase 4.6 acres of land bordering the east side of the church property. The additional land was purchased with growth in mind.

IX

Eat, Drink & Be Merry

Rockne's Pub on Hudson Drive is a popular place for a sandwich and "suds". In the early 1900s this ancient building was used as crew's quarters for the interurbans and streetcars.

Riverfront Centre District

Downtown Cuyahoga Falls is the site of numerous festivals and activities. On weekends, from May to October, pedestrians take over Front Street from Broad Boulevard to Portage Trail.

Events include the Crooked River Festival, the Oktoberfest, the Italian American Festival, the Blues, Cruise & Food Festival, Friday evening Rockin' on the River concerts, a Rib Burn Off, and many other merrymaking activities. The designated area is a perfect place to get together with friends.

Pontoon boat tours of the Cuyahoga River take place daily during seasonal weather. Boat captains and volunteer guides entertain and give passengers a different perspective of the city.

In the 1970s the city halted the flow of vehicle traffic on Front Street by constructing a pedestrian mall. Hoping to improve the festival area, in the late 1990s, the city hired consultants and spent nearly $600,000 on developing a plan designed to make the riverfront more community friendly.

In 2002, after much controversy, City Council finally approved $4.7 million for the construction of a permanent festival site on the riverfront. The plans call for an amphitheater, skating rink, fountain, and festival pavilion. It is hoped that the new festival site will attract even more people to the riverfront than in the past.

Marj Schlaeppi is the editor of the *Riverfront Rattler,* a quarterly newsletter distributed to the people who live, shop and work in the mall area. The Riverfront Centre Association meets monthly to discuss and plan events. Cuyahoga Falls Development Department, the Cuyahoga Falls Jaycees and the Riverfront Centre Association work together to provide programs that entertain and serve the public.

~

188

Sheraton Suites

Imagine "home away from home" at Sheraton Suites, with cantilevered decks that jut out over the cascading river. Floor to ceiling windows give diners a spectacular view of the rugged terrain. *Lodging Hospitality Magazine* named the Cuyahoga Falls hotel one of the top 40 suburban hotels in America. The NFO World Group specializing in research-based marketing has rated the Sheraton Suites #1 in Customer Service in Sheraton Hotels of North America.

Riverside Community Urban Redevelopment Corporation (RCURC) begins clearing land for construction of the Sheraton Suites in the late 1980s.
Photos Courtesy of Sheraton Suites.

Riverside Community Urban Redevelopment Corporation (RCURC), under the leadership of developer, Thomas J. Dillon and the architectural firm of Curtis & Rasmussen Inc., built the beautiful facility. Dillon had considered developing the plot of land in the early 1980s, but interest rates were extremely high, and he decided against the project at that time.

However, by 1987 the investment group was formed, and the project moved ahead under the leadership of Tom Dillon. A graduate of Akron University, Dillon had built numerous houses, hotels, banks, libraries, churches, schools and factories in the United States. His company merged with Forest City, and he gained international recognition building 33 sixteen-story buildings plus a factory in Iran. He created the "Dillon System" using manufactured mechanical and precast components, and poured in-place concrete.

Developer Tom Dillon, in dark work-jacket and hardhat, assists in pouring cement at the construction site of Sheraton Suites in 1989.

Other investors in RCURC included Abe J. Moses of Northampton, Massachusetts. Moses had been involved in organizing, directing and financing major development projects worldwide; Akronite, Russell W. Fesler, electrical contractor and owner of Community Electric, Inc.; Byron W. Fry, executive with the Coca-Cola Bottling Company of Ohio; and Gene Fiocca of Akron, former Construction Coordinator at Forest City Dillon, Inc., and president of Rubber Associates, Inc. Together, this group changed the riverfront site from a literal wasteland to a special gathering place for hotel guests, businesses and social functions.

Ground was broken in September 1988 for the new hotel. It was decided that all guestrooms in this hotel would be *suites*. Instead of 470 regular guestrooms, there would be 214 guest suites. Conference and banquet facilities were planned. In fact, the first banquet was held in December 1989 while construction crews were still working. The first hotel guests were registered in January 1990.

Sheraton Suites nears completion with cantilevered dining room under construction.

The Vaughn Machinery Company, a manufacturer of industrial machine equipment and wire, occupied the site of the Sheraton Suites for almost 150 years. Owned by four generations of the Vaughn Family, it was the oldest operating business in Cuyahoga Falls when it closed in 1974.

Dillon worked with many architects in creating this special place on the river. Architect, Harold Rasmussen, of Cuyahoga Falls, worked hand in hand with Dillon as the work progressed. RCURC employed 100 men rather than sub-contracting the many jobs to be done.

With headwaters in Geauga County, the Cuyahoga River descends a total of 600 feet or an average of nine feet per mile - a fall comparable to Niagara Falls. Sheraton Suites, located on the former site of the Vaughn Machinery Company, provides guests with a spectacular view of the falling waters.

In addition to the amenities that are associated with large hotels, the Sheraton prides itself in the "Rock Elevator" which takes visitors to the gorge and a close-up view of the falling waters. From that location, the cantilevered dining room, the cascading Cuyahoga River and the view of the riverside of the large building can be seen. The hotel employees 180 full and part-time employees.

Art's Place
(formerly Marcel's Supper Club)

Art's Place, formerly Marcel's Supper Club, on State Road is a favorite Cuyahoga Falls restaurant that boasts homestyle cooking and *comfort food*. Owners David O'Brien and Donna Daulton have been at this location for 26 years.

There's a long-standing eatery at 2225 State Road that has served the community for over fifty years. Many years ago it was known as Housley's Tavern. From the 1950s until the 1980s, the restaurant was known as Marcel's Supper Club. The new owners kept the name for nearly five years before renaming the establishment Art's Place.

Owners, David O'Brien and Donna Daulton, who are brother and sister, come from a long line of restaurateurs. The former Art's Place, south of Akron, was a family business. O'Brien and Daulton have been at the Cuyahoga Falls location for twenty-six years.

The restaurant makes all soups *from scratch*. They pride themselves in serving *comfort food* with plenty of meat, potatoes and gravy.

Even with special desserts and homestyle cooking, Art's Place works at keeping prices under control. Banquet facilities are available for groups of up to 50 people. All items on the menu are available for carryout service.

~

Benito's

When Benito Antognoli bought the old building in 1965, it was said to be the oldest licensed drinking establishment in the county. Built in the 1880s, the tiny building scarcely held 100 patrons, but it was where music lovers would come to hear and participate in jazz.

A customer, A. D. Jones, built a piano bar in the narrow windowless room. It wasn't long before Red Shannon, who played the gutbucket (an upside-down washtub with broomstick and a G-string from a base fiddle), and some of his cronies on piano and horns began *Blues at Benito's.*

The ensemble grew with Mo Klippert, a former Goodyear Vice President, and the Rubber City Retreads, playing Dixieland jazz. Over the years the areas best musicians found their way to Benito's. The place had a reputation for impromptu performances by stand-in musicians.

That's Lew's Jazz Band was the house band from about 1985-2002. When the place closed, Lew at the age of 83, had been playing every weekend for 26 years at Benito's. Crowds of people jammed the place to hear Peggy Coyle sing with the *Mostly Blues Band.* Performers from the Carousel Dinner Theatre often stopped in for a late evening of singing and dancing.

Phyllis and Robert Lay purchased the business from Antognoli in 1998. The beloved music continued, and the bar was as popular as ever. But in 2000, Robert

Cogdeill, of Robert's Developers Inc., bought the property. An office building and warehouse would replace the timeworn little tavern. The music stopped, the doors were locked and Benito's at last was dark.

Benito Antognoli's place was where jazz music came alive from 1965-2002. Jazz fans were disappointed when the tavern doors were closed permanently. An office building is scheduled to replace the 120-year-old structure.

~

Hilarities Comedy Club
(Formerly the Ohio Theater)

The brochure says "Let Hilarities Turn Your Celebration Into A Unique Memorable Occasion." You're sure to have fun, laughs, good food and beverages, along with entertainment provided by some of the nation's best comedians.

Hilarities Comedy Club is located at 1546 State Road in the old Ohio Theater building. Actually, the building has been used for a variety of things over the years.

In the 1950s, Rev. Rex Humbard, of Calvary Temple (later to become the Cathedral of Tomorrow), purchased the vacant theater for $65,000 and held church there on a regular basis.

Later, The Embers, an upscale restaurant, occupied the building for nearly 15 years. Since the mid 1980s, Tannous Barakat has owned the property. The theater that seats up to 300 people is open six nights a week.

~

Kippy's Restaurant

Did you stand in line at one of the Kippy's Restaurants waiting for a seat at the counter or booth? Does your mouth water when you think about one of Kippy's juicy hamburgers smothered with onions?

Nineteen-year-old Bob Heath, and his mother Gail, opened the first Kippy's Restaurant in 1938 on Main Street in Akron, Ohio. The place was open 24 hours a day, seven days a week. Gail named the place Kippy's after a "Skippy" newspaper comic strip.

Big name stars, such as Pattie Page, the Ames Brothers and Dick Haymes, who came to Akron to perform at the Palace Theatre, found their way to Kippy's.

Although Bob was busy with the restaurant, he promoted professional boxing by founding the Century Boxing Club. With his wife, Virginia, and brother George, he owned and operated the Heathco Adjustable Awning Company from 1952 to 1999.

The Cuyahoga Falls Kippy's restaurant opened at 2100 Front Street in 1940. They eventually moved across the street, and were the last of the Kippy's to close in 1984.

Other Kippy's restaurants were located at Arlington Plaza in Akron and at the Norton Center. About 130 employees were needed to keep all four restaurants opened during peak times.

Kippy's restaurants were known for their "Biggy Burgers" long before "biggy size" became popular at the fast-food chains in the late 1990s. It was a family operated business with good service, good food, and great milkshakes!

~

Doc Brown's CANTEEN RESTAURANT & COFFEE SHOP located on State Road was a popular eating establishment in the 1940s & 1950s.

Postcard Photo Courtesy of Pete Mellinger

~

LeFever's River Grille

Elegant Casual Dining can be found on the west bank of the Cuyahoga River, at 2291 Riverfront Parkway. If you haven't been to LeFever's, you are missing one of the most interesting combinations of "then & now" in the downtown area.

197

Partners, Bob LeFever and Lou Farris, Jr., took a building that has historical significance and transformed it into an attractive restaurant. The old powerhouse, often referred to as the generator plant, with its base anchored in bedrock, was destroyed in the flood of 1913.

It was rebuilt and was the source of power for several industries along the riverbank. But eventually, with the changes made by the Ohio Edison dam, the old building was abandoned and fell into a state of disrepair.

Only a shell of the original generator plant remains as developer, Lou Farris, Jr., begins transforming the abandoned site in 1990. Who could imagine that one day a fine restaurant would be standing here?

Developer Farris began upgrading the old site in 1990. In 1998, he and LeFever became partners in what would become a *river-view* restaurant. LeFever comes from a long line of restaurateurs. His great-great grandfather operated a boarding house in Branson, Missouri, and the family has been in the hospitality business ever since.

The "Crane Room" ceiling is filled with antiquated iron remnants left over from the power house days. This main dining room sports balconies that overlook the dam and rushing waters of the Cuyahoga.

The restaurant seats 188, with banquet facilities accommodating 80 guests. During seasonable weather customers may choose to sit outside and enjoy the scenery.

LeFever's River Grille on Riverfront Parkway is situated on the site of an old generator plant. The building was abandoned and in a state of disrepair when developer Lou Farris, Jr., and restaurateur, Bob LeFever, turned it into an eating establishment featuring *Elegant Casual Dining.* Customers can view first hand a classic example of "then & now" on the banks of the Cuyahoga River.

Bars, Taverns & Saloons

From the days when a shot of whiskey *was good for what ails you* until today, folks have found relaxation in "watering holes" throughout the city. As in every city, some are neighborhood bars and others are recognized as a great place by outsiders.

Taverns, bars and saloons that come to mind are **Tommy's Café** owned by Tom Bruno on Front Street. Do you remember the **Pioneer Saloon**?

Sonny Kline was the proprietor at **Kline's**. Remember the **Tap Room** that also served as a bus stop for those going to Cleveland? **The Star of Italy** was a private club. The **Eagles** has been around for nearly a century now.

Willard Nastas sold the **Silver Swan** about 20 years ago to Jim Hummel. **Glen's** on Front Street is now called **Hunts' Bar & Grill. Laconis**, at 6th Street and Sackett Avenue, was originally a pizza shop owned by Don Laconi.

Wooton's Tavern, at Wyoga and Graham Roads, did a tremendous Sunday beer business, selling "carry-out" to those on their way to the park.

Frankie's Café was owned and operated by Frank Swartz. How about the **Chestnut Beer Garden**, the **Kit-Kat**, and the **Boulevard Tavern?** I'm sure you remember **Benito's Café,** famous for its jazz bands, and **Rockne's Pub** owned by Vern Simons.

In addition to those we have named, there have been many more over the years. Places where one could *quench his thirst and rub elbows with a buddy.*

X

Places Remembered

Clock Tower, Cemeteries,
Cathedral of Tomorrow, Auto Museum,

Mini Antique Auto Museum

The Mobil Gas Station at 1930 Front Street had two bays for servicing cars and attendants who filled tanks, checked oil and cleaned windshields. *Full Service* it was called. Today the cream colored building is a mini antique auto museum owned by Bill Clifford.

Clifford was the owner-operator of the Clifford Funeral Home just south of the service station on Front Street. When the gas station owners were ready to sell the property in the early 1970s, Clifford purchased it with the intention of adding more space to his funeral home parking lot.

Instead, he removed the car lifts, gas pumps, Mobile sign, and began using the building for storage of his *treasures*. His hobby of collecting automobile memorabilia finally had a home. His collection would be housed in the renovated Mobil Gas Station.

He has at least 25 antique cars, but because of limited space, only three autos are on display at a time. The *automobilia* nearly takes up the entire small museum. The walls are covered with enamel signs, license plates, posters, and advertising pieces. On display are gas pumps, service station signs, and a collection of practically anything with wheels - - pedal cars, bicycles, wagons, go-carts, and a surrey with a fringe on top.

Bill enjoys his hobby, and that's the way it should be. He delights in finding a new collectible and has gone as far as Florida to bring back the treasure. There are no regular hours for the facility, but if he is in the museum, he will gladly show you around. Generally, when special events are held on the Riverfront Centre Mall, Bill is happy to give visitors a tour of the mini museum.

Bill Clifford has at least 25 collectible automobiles and a variety of other auto related items that he shares with the public at the Mini Antique Auto Museum, a former gas station, on Front Street.

Photo Courtesy of Marty Clifford Shoemaker

* * *

Cathedral of Tomorrow
-now the home of Ernest Angley Ministries-
(Majority of the following information came from a seven part
series in *The Beacon Journal* dated January 1991)

The dome spanned 220 feet, there was a 168-foot
stage, and 5,400 seats filled the main auditorium. It had
200 beds in baby nurseries, and 60,000 people attended
the opening festivities in 1958.

The Cathedral of Tomorrow is an ever-present
landmark on State Road. How did this contemporary
building become a permanent structure in Cuyahoga
Falls?

A community that was noticeably conservative
watched the building of the spectacular modern structure.
They stood by and observed the beginning of a tower that
can be seen for miles around. And for 45 years they
watched with interest the rise and fall of the Humbard
Cathedral of Tomorrow Ministries.

In order to understand the history of the complex,
it is necessary to look at its founders. The oldest of six
children, Alpha Rex Emmanuel Humbard, was born in
1919 to traveling evangelists, Alpha and Martha Belle
Humbard.

Spreading the gospel throughout the United States,
the growing family lived in travel trailers and moved from
place to place. Rex married Maude Aimee Jones of Dallas,
Texas, in 1942 and continued to travel and evangelize
with family members.

Rex was ordained in 1943 through his father's
"Jesus Light of the World Inc." He firmly believed the
"Message of the revival circuit: Be born again. Be saved.
Keep away from the devil and his sinful temptations. Let
men be men, and women be women. And above all, keep
your family together, according to God's law."

Rex had seen a large circus tent that could easily be put up and taken down within a few hours. It seemed a practical way of accommodating crowds and relieving the staff of renting auditorium space in each city.

The Humbard organization purchased their first tent, one that could seat 6,000 people, for $21,000. In 1952 the tent was erected on the northeast side of the Akron Municipal Airport, and controversial faith healer, Kathryn Kuhlman, was invited to minister to the crowds.

Akron was ripe territory for many evangelistic campaigns due to the large Appalachian population that had moved here to work in the Akron rubber factories. It was here that Rex Humbard decided to plant roots.

He broke away from the traveling family and rented space for his first permanent ministry. He built up a large following of believers, and broadcast his television programs from the old Copley Theater on Copley Road. Eventually he purchased the vacant Ohio Theater on State Road for $65,000 (now the location of Hilarities Comedy Club). In 1953 he officially named his church the Calvary Temple.

As the congregation began to swell, it was necessary to look for room to expand. He located property at 2700 State Road, and purchased it for $140,000. The deal also included two houses on Portage Trail that would become homes for the families of Humbard and his brother-in-law, Wayne Jones.

Rex wanted to build a dome structure and hired the architectural firm of A. L. Salzman & Sons of Chicago to oversee the project. The projected cost was $2.1 million. In 1959 the corporate name was changed to Cathedral of Tomorrow Inc.

With successful television coverage, Humbard became an *electronic preacher* along with Jerry Falwell, Jimmy Swaggart, Jim Bakker, Oral Roberts, and others. Television ministry throughout the world was an admirable goal, although, very expensive to produce. By 1961 the Cathedral of Tomorrow was in need of a loan. Local banks refused, but Humbard found a way.

Through the Central States Pension Fund of the mob-influenced Teamsters Union a loan was acquired for $1.2 million. In 1991 *The Beacon Journal* wrote, "In 1961, organized religion met organized crime . . ." Humbard became friends with Teamsters' President, Jimmy Hoffa, who personally administered the pension fund.

The Cathedral borrowed additional money, and by the time the public was made aware of the transactions, the church owed the Teamsters $5.6 million.

In order to fund the television ministry, the Cathedral of Tomorrow Inc. got involved in what the government would eventually say were *"profit making businesses"*. In 1965 they purchased the Real Form Girdle Company of Brooklyn, the Unity Electronics of Elizabeth, New Jersey, and the Nassau Plastics and Wire of Brooklyn.

Other businesses included the Don M. Heskett Advertising Agency and Adcraft Typographers, Inc. In 1971 the church purchased Mackinac Island College, a 32-acre educational recreational facility. They paid $10 million to acquire a 70 year lease for Cascade Plaza, the office and hotel complex in downtown Akron, to Columbus developer, John W. Galbreath. In addition, the Cathedral began selling unsecured bonds and became involved in estate planning and annuities.

The television ministry was expanding, and personalities such as music star Pat Boone and others appeared on the stage at the Cathedral. The Cuyahoga Falls TV studio was one of the largest stage sets outside Hollywood, and *Parade Magazine* reported on the success of the programming,

In 1971 Humbard hired the M. W. Kelogg Company of Houston to begin construction of what was billed as

Ohio's tallest tower. The 494 foot tall concrete portion of the tower was erected in 22 days.

Plans included a theater, a revolving restaurant, an observation floor, and an antenna that would make the tower 42 feet higher than Cleveland's Terminal Tower. The planned 750 foot spire in Cuyahoga Falls was yet to be seen.

Traveling evangelist, Rex Humbard, came to Akron in 1952 and set up a tent at the Akron Municipal Airport. The community was a ready audience, and Humbard settled here, eventually building the CATHEDRAL OF TOMORROW at 2700 State Road. The building now houses the Ernest Angley Ministries and WBNX Television.

Postcard Photo Courtesy of Pete Mellinger

Even though Humbard was enthusiastic, the community was not. Neighbors and a radio station filed lawsuits. The local township officials had concerns, and by the beginning of the following year it was obvious that the tower would never be finished.

It stood empty without a tenant or purpose for years. Finally in 1989 the tower was purchased. It now serves as a platform for Krieger Communication.

Changes in the law concerning taxes began to influence the profitability of the Cathedral's business ventures. Taxes had to be paid, and the U. S. Securities and Exchange Commission sued the Cathedral Corporation for the selling of bonds.

It was necessary to begin liquidating in order to repay investors, or "partners", $12.5 million. In addition, back taxes were owed to Summit County. It appeared as though the Cathedral of Tomorrow had met its end due to financial difficulties.

However, by 1977, 61 nations and 500 TV stations were tuned into the Cathedral. Supporters were sending $1.2 million a month according to news reports. The Cathedral of Tomorrow changed its corporate name to Rex Humbard Foundation.

Humbard had moved to Boca Raton, Florida, in the early 1970s, and had become a "commuter pastor" flying weekends to Cuyahoga Falls. Brother-in-law, the Rev. Wayne Jones, handled the weekly business in Ohio.

In the 1970s several trips were made to foreign countries by the Humbard organization. The private Lockheed Electra airplane was accompanied by a chartered Boeing 707 that carried 61 tons of television equipment.

A survey of those who lived in the area during the Cathedral of Tomorrow years shows that there are those who believe that the operation was a sham. However, there are many people who faithfully followed Rex Humbard and are firm in their belief that he was a good person and true messenger of God.

Humbard eventually moved his ministry from the area. The Ernest Angley Ministries purchased the properties and now conducts services and television evangelism from the State Road location.

* * *

The Clock Tower

It rang out loud and clear when fire hit the community. The bell in the clock tower of the First United Methodist Church served as a fire bell, which signaled for all available hands to come and fight the fire.

Town folks regulated their schedules throughout the day by the sounds from the musical chimes coming from the tower in the late 1800s. There were no digital disposable watches, nor radio and television stations broadcasting the time of day every few minutes. Folks relied on the town clock.

Bill Brothers Machine Works on Water Street built the tower clock in 1864 when Abraham Lincoln was President. It was presented to the village and installed in the tower of the church by Israel James.

In 1920 the old wooden church was razed, and the new brick church was built with a tower to accommodate the clock. In 1970, after serving the community for over 100 years, the church replaced the ancient timepiece with an electric clock. The old clock was retired.

Some years later, J. R. Mortensen, President of the Cuyahoga Falls Historical Society, discovered the clock in the attic of the First United Methodist Church. With the help of Rev. Forrest Waller, and trustees of the church, it was moved to the Historical Society Museum in the Quirk Cultural Center.

In 1993, the Cuyahoga Falls Historical Society presented an idea to the Oktoberfest Committee for displaying the clock. The estimated cost for the project was $112,000.

Mike Paul, owner of Fidelity Clock Repair in Bath, Ohio, agreed to restore the clock, and install it in the tower that was to be built. The Cuyahoga Falls Oktoberfest Committee offered to pay for the restoration and installation of the clock.

A committee was formed to raise funds and move forward with the project. Members were: Lyle Forest, Bob Kerr, J. R. Mortensen, Harry Heath, Larry Brimlow, George Winkelmann, Sue Truby, Carol Morgan, Phil First, and Louise Wichert. The committee sold 746 commemorative bricks to be placed in the lower section of the tower.

The site was chosen and approved by city council. George Winkelmann, of the Team 4 Architect Company, drew up the plans. Jerry Welty, of Welty Building Corporation, served as the general contractor. Several of the sub-contractors offered to donate materials and services to the project.

Dick Hurley, of W. L. Tucker Supply Company, donated bricks. Duer Construction Company donated the cement blocks and did all the masonry work on the tower.

Other generous donations came from Warren Gibson, Mike Paul, George Winkelmann, Community Electric, Jerry Welty, Bob Kerr, The Valley Savings & Loan, and The River Front Centre Association.

The beautiful red brick clock tower stands near Broad Boulevard on the Riverfront Centre Mall. The 137-year-old timepiece was electrified in 2001. Visitors to the mall may view the inner workings of the clock through observation windows at the base of the tower.

The community no longer relies on the clock chimes to keep track of the hour, as was the custom decades ago. Today, we enjoy the history the structure represents, and have a sense of well being as we hear the melodious sounds coming from the tower.

A clock built by Bill Brothers Machine Shop was presented to the village when Abraham Lincoln was president of the United States. The clock was moved from place to place over the next century. With the help of a steering committee and numerous donations by community members and businesses, a new clock tower was erected at Riverfront Centre Mall. The137-year-old timepiece was electrified in 2001.

Cemeteries

Burial of the deceased, whether in a family plot or a public cemetery, reflects the customs of the cultural group and the situation surrounding the death. We have all read accounts of pioneer families who buried the deceased along the trail as they traveled westward.

Others set aside a parcel of land on their own property reserved for burial of family members. Some prefer to cremate the body, and others choose an above the ground mausoleum. Veterans of wars are memorialized through monuments and designated burial locations. And burial at sea is yet another method of *laying the body to rest.*

Many churches have small cemeteries on adjoining property. For the purpose of this book, three major cemeteries, Oakwood, Chestnut Hill and Northlawn will be discussed.

Oakwood Cemetery

Early settlers had used the East Side schoolyard as a burial ground. Finally, in 1838, Oakwood Cemetery was founded, and bodies buried in the schoolyard were transferred to Oakwood.

Stories are often told of graveyards where overgrown weeds, small critters and snakes have taken over the unattended burial grounds. A group of concerned women in Cuyahoga Falls felt strongly that Oakwood Cemetery was in dire need of attention. In 1888, they formed the Ladies Cemetery Association and began setting goals to spruce up the burial grounds.

The group held dinners to raise money and offered membership in the organization for fifty cents a year. In 1895 the Cemetery Association hired Jack Hatfield, for $3.00 a month, as its first sexton or superintendent. The construction of a beautiful chapel, complete with memorial windows, was underway by 1898.

The huge trees and lovely plantings make Oakwood one of the most attractive cemeteries in the area. Visitors can view *Poet's Hill* where monuments and graves of the Sill and Newberry founding families are located.

A special section of the cemetery is the resting-place for over 700 veterans, with an additional 17,000 gravesides located within the park-like setting.

The Ladies Cemetery Association may be the oldest active organization in the city. Presidents of the organization: 1888-Emma Heath; 1897-Elizabeth Freeman; 1901-Emma Heath; 1905-Belle Peebles; 1911-Elizabeth Freeman; 1928-Mrs. Billman; 1958-May Sigler; 1962-Mary Smith; 1967-Helen Hansen; 1969-Sylvia Jurgensen; 1971-Iris Sager; 1973-Marion Pearce; 1975-Irene Turley; 1977-Helen Marshall; 1984-Margery Skeels Smith; 1991-Susann Drbal.

The beautiful chapel at Oakwood Cemetery was built in 1898. The Ladies Cemetery Association may be the oldest active organization in the city. Founded in 1888, the group took on fund-raising, planting flowers and the beautification of the burial grounds.

Chestnut Hill Memorial Park

The administrative offices at Chestnut Hill Cemetery are directly across from the duck pond. Carl F. Graefe, ecologist and former owner, created an arboretum and filled the pond on the property with many species of fowl.

The quiet pond at the entrance of Chestnut Hill Memorial Park attracts visitors who come to feed the many species of ducks that live there year-round. A variety of flora among the majestic trees add to the beauty of the cemetery on Sackett Avenue. The 55-acre parcel of land was originally part of the 259-acre Joseph Babb Farm.

Real estate developer and ecologist, Carl F. Graefe, built an arboretum on the property in 1920. In 1924 the land became a memorial park. He later sold the cemetery to Akron's First United Church of Christ. Twelve years later, in 1998, The Loewen Group of Vancouver, British Columbia, purchased the cemetery. The Alderwood

Corporation of Cincinnati, Ohio, took possession of the property in 2002.

Currently there are approximately 5,800 gravesites in Chestnut Hill Memorial Park. Ample burial plots are available with 24 acres yet to be developed.

Northlawn Memorial Gardens

The spectacular "Avenue of Flags" on Memorial Day at Northlawn Cemetery is possible because of the donation of 480 flags donated by families of veterans.

Spaced forty feet apart, the billowing Stars and Stripes are a testimonial of the courage and valor of our fighting men. The flags were presented to families of servicemen by the government. Families then donated the flags to Northlawn for the purpose of being part of the special annual event.

Summit County resident, Mary Carr, and partners opened Northlawn Memorial Gardens Mausoleum and Crematory in 1961. In 1998 the cemetery at 4724 State Road was sold to Equity Corporation International. In 1999 Service Corporation International, the largest company in the industry, purchased the property.

Superintendent, Craig A. Smith, has been with Northlawn since 1978. There are approximately 50 acres available for burial purposes. Approximately 8,300 gravesites are presently on the premises, with an additional 400 spaces located in the mausoleums. It is expected that a total of 30,000 gravesites will completely fill Northlawn Memorial Gardens.

Veterans are remembered on Memorial Day at Northlawn Memorial Gardens with the display of 480 American flags donated by the families of Veterans.

* * *

Ascot Park

It seems that there has always been some kind of horse racing track within the Summit County area. Records indicate that a half-mile track was constructed at the Summit County Fairgrounds in 1856. At that time the fairgrounds were on South Main Street in Akron, not far from where the Aeros Baseball Stadium is today. Although the county fair location moved five times in the next 72 years, a racetrack was always a necessity.

Cuyahoga Falls had its own horse races right on Front Street in 1859. Although we don't know how well the races were attended, the Civil War was blamed for the discontinuation of the events.

The annual Northampton Homecoming, held at Iron Bridge School on the banks of Mud Brook, always featured buggy races down State Road. The event started at Chart Road and finished at the Iron Bridge. Again, another war caused the activity to be discontinued. This time, it was World War I.

Steve Steinmetz built a horseracing track in Northampton on the old Harrington farm in 1923. It was called Northampton Track. He sold the operation and the new owners changed the name to Ascot Park. In 1944 admission was just twenty-five cents. Large and more prestigious tracks elsewhere began to attract patrons. In 1968, with the track in a state of disrepair, the complex was demolished.

Today, a portion of the Ascot Industrial Park sits in the general area of the old racetrack.

Ascot Park, located in Northampton Township, was promoted as one of America's most beautiful three-quarter mile racetracks. The site of a 43-day thoroughbred meet each summer. The old dilapidated complex was demolished in 1968.
Postcard Picture Courtesy of Pete Mellinger

Akron Institute
(Formerly Falls Medical Building)

In 1959 a group of Cuyahoga Falls physicians formed Port-Haven Associates, Inc. Headed by Dr. Fred Somma, the group hired Kamenir-Hamed Architects to design a modern medical facility at 1625 Portage Trail.

By 1962 the building was underway with features that seemed futuristic for the times. Akron Savings & Loan financed the project, and the Ernest Alessio Construction Company was hired to build the $1,100,000 structure.

The 85-foot diameter circular building is four stories tall with an additional story below ground for mechanical equipment and additional suites. Exterior walls above the first floor are of reinforced concrete pre-cast panels.

Exterior walls of reinforced concrete pre-cast panels made the circular building on Portage Trail modernistic in 1962. Originally built by a group of medical professionals, the building now houses the Akron Institute, a training facility.

Twenty-two suites are built around a central reinforced concrete core supported by exterior columns. The upper floors cantilever out eight feet. Elevators, restrooms, heating, cooling, and plumbing are contained in the core. A single corridor rings the entire building at each level.

In 1996 the Akron Institute, formerly known as the Akron Medical-Dental Institute, moved to the old medical building on Portage Trail. Akron Institute was founded in 1970.

It is owned by North American Training Services, Inc., a corporation, and is accredited by the Accrediting Commission of Career Schools and Colleges of Technology (ACCSCT).

The institute provides training in the areas of medical assistants, dental assistants, medical billing assistants, and network technologists. David L. LaRue serves as director of the Akron Institute.

* * *

Dance instructor Charles Boyd last occupied the circa-1845 Greek Revival house on Third Street. One of the oldest remaining houses in the city; it is scheduled for demolition to make way for the new Natatorium.

XI
Memories from the Past

Narratives

Listening to the voices of those who have lived a lifetime in Cuyahoga Falls gives us a glimpse into history of the area. Their recollections of places, times and events help us to understand the changes that have taken place. The nostalgia intertwined in the stories they tell gives flavor to the cold hard facts of community development.

Harding Wichert came to Cuyahoga Falls in 1933 after attending thirteen different schools while his father supported the family in the construction trade throughout the United States. An aunt shared living space with the young family in a house on 2nd Street while Harding's dad trained to become an insurance agent.

Harding recalls watching pennies being flattened on the trolley car tracks in the middle of town as the noisy trains rolled by. He considered himself a good swimmer having moved here from New Rochelle, New York, and swimming in the Atlantic Ocean. So, when the boys of his neighborhood asked him to go swimming at the local swimming hole, Harding was anxious to join the group. However, Harding says he nearly drowned in the muddy dirt pond we now call Water Works Park.

Ambitious Harding delivered the <u>Cleveland Plain Dealer,</u> a morning paper, and then later on in the day

219

delivered the afternoon edition of the <u>Akron Times Press</u> to the residents of the Falls. When he had the use of a car, he operated a dry cleaning route in Cuyahoga Falls and Stow.

Harding recalls the names of memorable high school instructors including musical arts teacher Josephine Long, Dr. George Erf in the chemistry department. J. A. Gerberick, a German instructor and strict disciplinarian, and history teacher Gilbert Roberts, who later became principal of the school

Harding graduated from Cuyahoga Falls High School in 1939 and was soon drafted into the United States Armed Forces. His wife, Louise Klespies Wichert, who had been banking her salary plus the money Harding sent home, surprised him with the purchase of a new home on Birchwood Avenue when he returned from Germany.

Wichert was the Mayor of Cuyahoga Falls from 1952-53. He says the monthly wage for the job of running the city was a whopping $250. He received a pay raise before the end of his term that guaranteed him $500 a month. He recalls housing developer, Fred Heslop, building hundreds of homes in the Falls including those on the east side of the river or the "Canadian" side, in a section of the city often referred to as tobacco row.

Harding followed his father into the insurance agency business and eventually turned the successful third generation operation over to his son, Thomas Harding Wichert.

Harding Wichert – 2001

Marion Orth Pearce was born in 1909 in a house on 3rd Street where the Natatorium now stands. She spent some of her early years in a house on Broad Boulevard that was demolished to make way for the library. She raised three daughters in Cuyahoga Falls and now lives at Silver Lake Towers.

Marion's parents came to Cuyahoga Falls from Port Clinton, Ohio, in 1905. Frank William Orth owned the local newspaper, *The Cuyahoga Falls Reporter*, with a partner for a short time. He eventually owned and operated the F. W. Orth Printing Company located in Cuyahoga Falls.

Marion recalls going shopping for her mother by taking the dirt path that ran diagonally from 3rd and Stow Streets to 2nd and Portage Trail. Fresh cut meat could be purchased at Snook's Meat Market. One never went to the south end of Front Street where the saloons were located, and the drunks might be "whirling around". Shopping was done at the north end of the block

She recalls singing "Nothing But A Big Wax Doll" when she was about 5 years old (1914) on the stage of an auditorium on 2nd Street. Marion's Cuyahoga Falls High School graduating class of 1927 was the first class to attend the new building all four years. She remembers too, that it was customary on Decoration Day (Memorial Day), for every school child to march in the parade. They carried handfuls of flowers to place on soldiers' graves at Oakwood Cemetery.

Marion's mother thought that she had "arrived" when asked to serve on the Oakwood Cemetery Board. Today, Marion, two of her daughters and a granddaughter, are Board members.

She remembers that her two brothers and a few other young men in the community rented the old Vaughn mansion. They formed the "Coppacaw Club" for boys – no girls allowed. She also recalls a story about a group of boys who skipped going to church on North Front Street, and instead, collected snakes near the river. Folks said that the snake pile was four feet high by the time church was over.

Marion says she loves Cuyahoga Falls and would like to win the lottery and build an auditorium for the community. She says she would name it Orth Auditorium in honor of her parents.

Marion Orth Pearce – 2001

Lila VanSweringen, the country girl from Nebraska, met husband Ted in Washington State, where he was stationed while in the United States Air Force. When he was discharged they moved to Ted's hometown, Greensburg, Ohio. They eventually bought a house on 27th Street in Cuyahoga Falls in what Lila lovingly refers to as *Heslop's Hatchery* (a place where numerous children were born to the young families living in the development). The VanSweringen's had sons Bryan, born in 1953, and Mark, born in 1955.

Lila serves on the Taylor Library Board, plays the piano, is an avid fan of the Cuyahoga Falls High School Tiger's, and is a contributing poet and member of the International Society of Poets.

Lila recalls working for the Goodyear Tire and Rubber in the Store Planning & Display Department, when she first arrived in Ohio. However, her favorite job was in the Superintendent's office of the Cuyahoga Falls City School District.

In that position she observed many changes that took place within the city and school system. She remembers that at one time the student population in the Cuyahoga Falls City School District was 12,069, and when she retired in 1988 after 24 years with the district, the student enrollment was less than 6,000.

She recalls that Superintendent Harold Wilson said that the district would not sell vacant school buildings, but would lease them for $1 per year. She watched as Grant School became the Quirk Cultural Center, Schnee Elementary became the YMCA, and Bode Elementary School was leased to Goodyear Tire and Rubber Company

222

for a training facility, and now serves as the Summit County Educational Resource Center.

Lila watched as Crawford and Broad Elementary Schools were demolished. She recalls that in 1965 the Silver Lake School District became part of the Cuyahoga Falls District. During her years in the Superintendent's office, Roberts Middle and DeWitt Elementary Schools were built. She remembers working in 1978 with Martha Leach, of Kettering, Ohio, to help found the Ohio Branch of the Educational Office Professionals.

Lila had a bumper sticker that she donated to the Cuyahoga Falls Historical Society that said that Cuyahoga Falls was one of the 24 best places in the United States to live. She is happy that she made this city her home.

Lila VanSweringen - 2002

William Louis Parthe graduated from Cuyahoga Falls High School in 1949 and received a Geology Degree from Miami University. He was the Commanding Officer on the Navel Ship USS Hollidaysburg serving in the Great Lakes area. He has had a variety of interests and careers that include owning a business, showing horses, working as a sales representative, and earning a living plucking the strings of a banjo.

Bill recalls taking piano lessons as a kid from Miss McDade, a teacher at Broad Street Elementary School. In high school he was a member of "Willie Tripp & the Stumblers" band. The group played at school functions and at Simler's Tavern. He remembers "Pop Erf", a favorite chemistry teacher. His mother, Dora, was the secretary for Cuyahoga Falls Mayor Elmer Wolf, and Bill was a charter member of Cuyahoga Falls Demolay.

In the mid-1960's, Bill won a banjo in a sales promotion contest where he was employed. He taught himself to play the prized instrument and eventually was supplementing his income playing Dixieland jazz. He recalls giving banjo lessons in Hudson where Art Freeman, the Director of Entertainment at Sea World, was a student. That contact led to a 25-year relationship with the amusement park. Strolling through the park and playing for pre-show audiences, Parthe was a favorite with the crowds.

Bill and his banjo are regulars at the annual Cuyahoga Falls Oktoberfest. In addition, his group has entertained at the Bowery on West Market Street in Akron, now called Nickelby's Lounge, and at the Covered Bridge in Bath. He has been a member of the Hymns of Dixie, Earlville Jazz Band and the River City Jazz Band for several years.

William Louis Parthe – 2002

Patricia Bauman Gritton is an octogenarian, who was possibly the first woman die maker in the nation. As a child, she hovered about as her dad, Paul Bauman, owner of Bauman Steel Rule Cutting Dies, created dies to be used nationwide.

Paul Bauman worked at Falls Paper Box Company, but had learned his trade at the Fort Wayne Paper Box Company in Indiana. He opened his own shop in 1927 on the second floor of a building on Front Street, next to the old City Hall. The business was moved to Vincent Street where it existed until 1997.

Patricia graduated from Cuyahoga Falls High School and worked at Taylor Memorial Library. But, she had learned the die building trade, and she was destined to take over her father's business.

Patricia recalls working with her dad until his death in 1956. They made dies for a variety of children's items. Saafield Publishing Company hired Bauman Steel to create the dies for jigsaw puzzles. She remembers the

224

Shirley Temple paper doll cutout books and the classic black and white silhouettes that required steel dies.

One of the most intriguing jobs involved making the dies for the first astronauts' suits. In fact, Bauman Steel Rule Cutting Dies received special recognition from NASA in 1962 for participation in the space program. She also recalls Russ Colley, a B. F. Goodrich employee and Cuyahoga Falls neighbor, who was one of the designers of the space suit.

Patricia remembers bringing her husband, Bob Gritton, into the business full time in 1958. He passed away in 1983, but Patricia continued to operate the long-standing business. Contracts with the Soap Box Derby and Ace Rubber kept her busy.

As Patricia approached her 80th birthday she began thinking about retirement. There were no children in the Bauman household to take over the business. So in 1997, the machinery was sold, and the business history was given to Kent State Library archives. Bauman Steel Rule Cutting Dies had been in business in the Cuyahoga Falls area for 70 years.

Patricia Bauman Gritton - 2002

Floriana Berdyck Hall was honored June 1, 2002, as a Distinguished Alumni of Cuyahoga Falls High School. Floriana graduated in 1945, and although she has always written poetry, it wasn't until around 1996 that she was recognized nationally for her talent.

She started the *Poet's Nook*, a poetry group that meets at Taylor Memorial Library. She has been honored in *Who's Who In U. S. Writers, Editors & Poets*, and *Who's Who In Poetry*.

Daughter of Floriana, and a rascal of a father, Francis, Floriana attended 10 different schools before enrolling at Cuyahoga Falls High School. Floriana has two younger brothers.

Floriana recalls the desperate situation when the family had little to eat and Francis would be gone for weeks at a time. A sandwich of lard and sugar was not a substitute for a good meal. She didn't let her school chums know of the unfortunate situation, and the family found out years later that Francis was often absent because he had another family.

She recalls being selected, because of her secretarial skills, by a "scout" from General Tire Rubber Company. She was hired at 17 years of age, and paid $50 per week, to work for the major firm. Eighty percent of her paycheck went to her mother to help support the family.

Floriana met husband, Robert, at Summit Beach Park. They were married on New Year's Eve, 1948. They have 5 children and 11 grandchildren.

Floriana is inspired to write poetry and autobiographical stories based upon her life.

Floriana Hall - 2002

H. F. Mellinger Jr. (Pete) has been interested and involved in the history of Cuyahoga Falls all of his life. His dad was a Charter Member of the Cuyahoga Falls Historical Society, and Pete is active in the organization today. Pete has a large collection of Cuyahoga Falls memorabilia.

Pete was a member of the June 1951 graduating class of Cuyahoga Falls High School. That class still meets, 51 years later, on a monthly basis, for breakfast. Pete retired from Goodyear Tire and Rubber Company after 40 years and has been married to Barbara Gould Mellinger since 1982.

Pete recalls playing on the road grading equipment parked at Smith's Supply Company. He kept track of the time by the gigantic clock on the Falls Lumber Company building. If he wasn't home on time, his parents accepted no excuses. In high school, Pete recalls going with his buddies, during lunch hour, to Oakwood Cemetery and sitting among the tombstones eating lunch.

He recalls riding his tricycle in the Cuyahoga Falls 125th Anniversary celebration parade. And for the 150th Anniversary, he was a "Brother of the Brush" growing a beard for the special event. During the City's 175th Anniversary, Charles Boyd served as Grand Marshall of the Parade, and Pete was involved in an Arts & Crafts show.

Pete wonders what happened to the large sign that stood at Broad Boulevard and 2nd Street in the 1940s. The names of all members of the community who were serving in the military during World War II were posted there.

He enjoyed growing up in Cuyahoga Falls and continues to be fascinated with the history of the area.

Pete Mellinger – 2002

Dorothy Season Wright is a member of society whose family roots are deeply planted in the history of Cuyahoga Falls. Grandfather, W. W. Warner, who was an abstractor, was responsible for allotting the Duncan farm property that stood between 4th and 6th Streets.

He, along with three of his children, then built the first houses on 6th Street (then called Allen Street). Dorothy's father, Archie B. Season, graduated from Cuyahoga Falls High School in 1895. He served on many city government committees and worked for the school district.

Dorothy graduated from Cuyahoga Falls High School in 1935, and attended Kent State University majoring in Education. She taught at Richardson and Schnee Elementary Schools.

Dorothy's first husband, E. C. Shingleton, died at the age of 52. Dorothy later married W. Richard Wright. She has two daughters.

227

Dorothy remembers when Broad Boulevard ended at 7th street. Only woods and a stream stood in the area that is now 13th Street. Second Street was lined with beautiful Victorian Style homes. She was never allowed to go down to the river's edge because of the danger. However, she does recall roller-skating on walks that were made of flagstone rather than cement.

Because of the Great Depression, Cuyahoga Falls Schools were closed the year that Dorothy was a sophomore. There was not enough money to continue operating; therefore, the School Board made the decision to shut the doors. School did not reopen until the following fall, and at that time the lost months had to be made up. A side note: there is not a 1935 yearbook because of the school-closing situation.

Dorothy recalls the businesses on Front Street that included an Arcade, the Alhambra Theater and Mitchell's Dry Goods Store. She has many good memories of her life in Cuyahoga Falls.

Dorothy Seasons Wright – 2002

Bee and **Walt McLean** have lived in Cuyahoga Falls so long that they can remember when Chestnut Boulevard ended at 3rd Street. Actually, Walt has lived here for 91 years. And Bee Starkey came with her family from Ravenna, Ohio, when she was two years old, 86 years ago.

Walt graduated from Cuyahoga Falls High School in 1929. He attended Akron University and worked at General Tire and Rubber Company. Bee graduated in the Cuyahoga Falls High School January 1931 class, and attended Actual Business College. The McLeans have four children and have been married for 66 years.

They recall that they were on their way to Water Works Park for a picnic in 1940, when the Doodlebug train collided with a 73-car freight train. The accident scene was one they will never forget. They also remember that at

228

one time the fire station was located at the corner of Front Street and Broad Boulevard. However, the horses were in a barn on 2nd Street, about where St. Joseph School is today. When the fire whistle sounded, if Bee ran as fast as she could, she likely would see the horses tearing down the street toward the waiting fire wagon.

As kids, they enjoyed sledding down Portage Trail when the city would close the roadway to automobile traffic. Cinders were spread on the road in front of the railroad tracks so children and sleds would be stopped.

The old post office was located just east of the river on Portage Trail. There were two mail deliveries daily. And mail was always delivered Christmas morning so that everyone was assured of getting last minute Christmas cards. (By the way, postage was 2 cents for first class mail.)

Bee recalls that her dad worked as a finish carpenter for Hoiles & Hedden, contractors who built many houses on the west side of town. She remembers "Church School" for elementary age school children. With parents' permission, children were allowed to leave school on Wednesday afternoon and attend special classes at one of the big churches on church square.

Saturday night "in town" on Front Street was a big affair. In those days, that is where everyone spent Saturday evenings.

Walt's grandfather lived in Alliance, Ohio. The family frequently rode the interurban all the way to Alliance for a visit. It involved riding three interurbans. First going through Akron, and then Canton, and finally arriving at grand-dad's place several hours later.

The McLeans have remarkable recall concerning places, events and their 85+ years living in Cuyahoga Falls.

Bee and Walt McClean – 2002

Those who have been around for a while remember Tip's Market at Barney's Busy Corner
Photo Courtesy of Pete Mellinger

XII

Trivia & Tales to Consider

We have heard these stories and perhaps you have heard them too. Some we know to be true, others are tales to be considered.

- The first Pontoon Boat River Trip took place in 1984 after Mr. Emil Czetli, a member of the Oktoberfest Committee, approached the Parks & Recreation Department with the idea.
- Cuyahoga Falls was originally called Manchester.
- The *original* falls, somewhere between the Sheraton Suites and the Ohio Edison Dam, cannot be seen.
- Cuyahoga Falls is made up of property from four townships; Stow, Northampton, Tallmadge and Portage.
- In 1830 Cuyahoga Falls had the only paper mill west of the Allegheny Mountains.
- The Portage Trail water storage tank, across from Bolich Middle School, holds 2 million gallons of water.
- There are *at least* 5,203 streetlights, 77 traffic lights and 1,551 fire hydrants in the city.
- Riverfront Centre, formerly called the Front Street Mall, was completed in 1977.
- The Natatorium originally had a "bubble" roof.
- The planting of daisies is forbidden in Oakwood Cemetery because in the days of horse-drawn funeral processions, the horses would stop to eat the daises.
- The Oakwood Cemetery office was used to store caskets during the winter months when the ground was frozen and it was impossible to hand dig graves.
- On July 31, 1940, forty-three passengers died when the *Doodlebug* shuttle from Hudson to Akron collided with a 73-car freight train near Front Street and Hudson Drive.
- The tallest tulip tree in Cuyahoga Falls is located in the 2300 block of Chestnut Boulevard.
- North Hill was called Summit City and earned the name *The Chuckery* because of a canal project, and the population of one man and 9,999 woodchucks.
- Northampton once had a distillery that made whiskey from potatoes.

- In 1882, the Central Union Telephone Company established the first telephone service with 35 subscribers and a switchboard located in the rear of Mercer Drug Store on Front Street.
- In 1940 Mr. and Mrs. Hugh A. Galt gave the city 16 acres of land to be used for "playground and recreational purposes" – Galt Park.
- The orchestra at the Silver Lake ballroom played from a platform suspended above the dance floor.
- Snakes always seemed to be a problem in the town of Cuyahoga Falls.
- Blossom Music Center is the summer home of the Cleveland Orchestra.
- More females than males live in Cuyahoga Falls.
- Residents of Cuyahoga Falls pay less for utilities than surrounding communities.
- Not all Italians live in the North Hill section of Akron – Cuyahoga Falls has its own *Little Italy*.
- Sheraton Suites Hotel has no hotel rooms, only hotel suites.
- Cuyahoga Falls Alumni Association has a list of 29,000 Cuyahoga Falls High School graduates.
- In his will, dance instructor, Charles Boyd, left the majority of the contents of his house to the Cuyahoga Falls Historical Society.
- Ray Heslop built "Heslopville" in Cuyahoga Falls with the construction of hundreds of affordable houses.
- In the early 1800s, William Wetmore Jr. "got taken with temperance" and took away the keg of whiskey he furnished for his employees each week.
- On March 6, 1858, temperance workers staged a "whiskey riot" in Cuyahoga Falls.
- Many fine artists settled in the area because they found work in the commercial departments of the major rubber companies.
- Once upon a time the Cuyahoga River *caught on fire*.

Bibliography and Suggested Reading

A Centennial History of Akron 1825-1925. The Summit County Historical Society, 1925

A History Of The Town of Cuyahoga Falls, Summit County, Ohio. Cleveland Herald Press

Akron Beacon Journal. Knight Ridder Publishers

Bierce, General L.V. *Historical Reminiscences of Summit County.* T. & H. C. Canfield Publishers, 1854

Bloetscher, Virginia Chase. *Indians Of The Cuyahoga Valley and Vicinity.* Cuyahoga Valley Archaeological Society, 1997

Blower, James M. & Korach, Robert S. *The NOT&L Story.* Central Electric Railfan's Association, 1966

Christiansen, Harry. *Northern Ohio's Interurbans and Rapid Transit Railways.* Transit Data, Inc., 1965

Cuyahoga Falls 1812-1987, 175th Anniversary. Published by the 175th Anniversary Commemorative Book Committee, Cuyahoga Falls, Ohio 1987

Cuyahoga Falls News-Press. Record Publishing Company

Ellis, William Donohue. *The Cuyahoga.* Landfall Press, Inc., 1998

Grismer, Karl H. *Akron and Summit County.* Summit County Historical Society, 1952

Guide to Ohio Newspapers 1793-1973. Edited by Stephen Gutgesell, Ohio Historical Society, 1974

Hatcher, Harlan. *The Western Reserve.* The World Publishing Company, 1949

Knepper, George W. *Ohio and Its People.* Kent State University Press, 1997

Mathews, Alfred, *Ohio and Her Western Reserve.* Heritage Books, Inc., 2001, Reprint from 1902

Seguin, Marilyn & Scott. *Images of America Cuyahoga Falls, Ohio.* Arcadia Publishing, 2000

The 1962 Cuyahogan. Cuyahoga Falls High School Year Book, 1962

The Coppacaw Story, A History of Cuyahoga Falls. Edited by Calvin W. Heintz, Published by the Sesquicentennial Committee, 1962

Times Press. Knight Ridder Publishers

INDEX

INDEX

236

INDEX

INDEX

INDEX

For membership in the organization and additional information about Cuyahoga Falls, contact the CUYAHOGA FALLS HISTORICAL SOCIETY – P.O. Box 186, Cuyahoga Falls, Ohio 44222